P9-BYM-974

EGYPTIAN PHARAOHS

EGYPTIAN PHARAOHS

3,000 YEARS OF DYNASTIC RULE

MARTIN HOWARD

FALL RIVER PRESS

This 2009 edition published by
Fall River Press, by arrangement with
Compendium Publishing Ltd.

Project manager: Ray Bonds
Designer: Cara Rogers
Picture research: Jo St Mart
Color Reproduction: Anorax Imaging Ltd

Fall River Press
122 Fifth Avenue
New York, NY 10011

ISBN 13: 978-1-4351-0407-5
ISBN 10: 1-4351-0407-2

Printed and bound in China

1 3 5 7 9 10 8 6 4 2

Additional illustrations

Page 1: Smendes, first pharaoh of the 21st Dynasty. *(The Art Archive/Egyptian Museum, Cairo/Alfredo Dagli Orti/AA326325)*

Pages 2-3: Remains of Khafre's pyramid. *(Jo St Mart)*

Pages 4-5: Mentuhotep I wearing the high white crown of Upper Egypt. *(Jo St Mart)*

Contents

Introduction

Commanding wealth and power beyond anything seen in the ancient civilizations until the rise of mighty Persia, the kings and queens of Ancient Egypt were truly as gods on Earth. Exalted as divine by the peoples they ruled over, the pharaohs were believed to be the living incarnation of Horus, the falcon god, whose own father was Osiris, the divine king. As such, he or she (as we will see, there were a number of female pharaohs) held the power of life and death over Egypt's peoples and had absolute control over the land and all it produced, as well as being supreme military commander of the country's armies.

There is still an enormous amount that we do not understand about Ancient Egypt and its rulers. Century upon century of neglect and decay have taken much knowledge that might have illuminated—not to mention the depredations of grave robbers and masons eager to recycle the silent tombs of Ancient Egypt's monarchs. Yet the artifacts that we do have, interpreted over the years by historians and archeologists, speak of an extraordinary race of people. Artistically and culturally like none other seen before or since, they pioneered advanced mathematical systems, construction techniques that are still not fully comprehended, medicine, irrigation and other agricultural advances, and writing systems that produced a great body of literature, and left behind treasures of art and architecture that still have the power to inspire awe.

Left: This ornately decorated golden fan was once one of many ceremonial fans belonging to Tutenkhamun. (*Jo St Mart*)

Right: Much of what we know about Ancient Egypt's history comes from the examination of mummies and the artifacts found with them. This painted limestone decoration from the tomb of Amenhotep III and Amenhotep IV at Asasif, Thebes, shows mourners at the feet of bandaged mummies of Nebamun and Ipuky. (*The Art Archive/Gianni Dagli Orti/AA365463*)

But above all this stands the figure of the pharaoh, bestriding 3,000 years of Ancient Egyptian civilization like a Colossus. Perhaps more than any other monarch in history the pharaoh and his land were united. The pharaoh was Egypt's link to the gods, its king, its government, and its instrument of retribution against enemies. It is impossible to underestimate the extent to which the pharaoh, sponsor of the arts and source of inspiration, directly shaped Ancient Egypt's history.

Such power as the pharaoh's is perhaps difficult to conceive of today, but can be illustrated through comparison of a single structure—the Great Pyramid of Khufu (or Giza)—with another famous prehistoric construction built about the same time (2500 BCE), Stonehenge in southern England. Stonehenge consisted of approximately a hundred roughly shaped stones, the largest of which weighed no

Below: The sphinx has stood guard over the towering pyramids of Giza since the reign of Khafre although recently it has begun to erode thanks to the harsh conditions of the desert. *(Jo St Mart)*

more than forty-five tons. Rightly so, it is regarded as an astonishing achievement for those early Britons who built it, yet Stonehenge is literally dwarfed by the breathtaking scale and perfection of the Great Pyramid. Computer analysis suggests that about 2,300,000 precisely cut stones were used in the initial construction, the largest of which weighed in at seventy tons. These were faced with a further 150,000 casing stones, each of which was highly polished and flat to within 1/100ths of an inch. When fixed they would have been placed with an accuracy of 5/1000ths of an inch, with an exact 2/100ths of an inch left for mortar. It is worth mentioning that, although we can now analyze the chemical

Above: The giant statues of Ramesses II at Abu Simbel. Carved from the natural sandstone, these enormous figures were buried under the sand until their discovery in 1813. (*Jo St Mart*)

composition of the mortar used, even with modern technology no one has been able to replicate it; it is harder than the stones themselves.

As others have noted, it would be possible to comfortably fit within the Great Pyramid the cathedrals of Florence, Milan, and Rome (St. Peter's), as well as London's St. Paul's Cathedral and Westminster Abbey, with room to spare. And the Great Pyramid is just one structure in a land

Right: High in the cliff face lies the tomb of the Persian king, Artaxerxes. During his rule he acquired a nickname, Macrochier, which roughly translated means "one arm longer than the other." (*Jo St Mart*)

Far right: The kiosk of Nectanebo I situated on the sacred island of Philae was just one of the pharaoh's many achievements. (*Jo St Mart*)

teeming with incredible tombs, temples, and statues, each built at the pharaoh's command and at his expense.

Today, well over 5,000 years after the first of these god-kings established a capital at Memphis, many of their names continue to ring down the ages: Amenhotep, Thutmose, Ramesses, Tutankhamun and more are the stuff of legend and wonder. But there are others among the 170 pharaohs that we know of whose lives and deeds are less famous. Their mysteries, riches, and hubris can be glimpsed in the relics they left behind, monuments to a culture that spanned millennia and which is almost entirely alien to us now. It is the intention of this book to delve into Egypt's past, into its tombs and splendors, to chart the rise and fall of Ancient Egypt through the monarchs that were at the nation's very heart, both those whose names are known to every schoolchild, and those who are less familiar.

DYNASTIES AND KINGDOMS

When uncovering almost 3,000 years of history it is important to have a framework within which to navigate. That used today is based upon the work of the Greek-Egyptian priest Manetho, whose *Egyptian History* (written in the 3rd century BCE) carved the millennia of Ancient Egypt into shorter periods. Manetho chose the appropriate and simple method of denoting periods by the different ruling houses—or dynasties—dating from the unification of Upper and Lower Egypt in circa 3100 BCE to the death of the final native Egyptian pharaoh (Nectanebo II, in 343 BCE). This gives thirty chronological dynasties, including a period of Nubian dominance (25th Dynasty, 747–656 BCE) and one of Persian (First Persian Period, 27th Dynasty, 525–404 BCE). A further two are commonly added, namely the Second Persian Period of 343–332 BCE (31st Dynasty),

and a final era following the conquest of Egypt by Alexander the Great in 332, through the Ptolemaic rulers, and ending with the suicide of Cleopatra VII in 30 BCE (32nd Dynasty).

More broadly, Ancient Egypt's history is broken down into "Kingdoms" denoting periods of stability, separated by "Intermediate" eras of political turmoil. These are known as the Old Kingdom (2686–2181 BCE), the Middle Kingdom (2040–1782 BCE), and the New Kingdom (1570–1070 BCE). Bookending the sweep of Egyptian history contained within the three kingdoms are two further eras, the Early Dynastic Period of 3150–2686 BCE and the Late Period of 525–332 BCE. Beyond the latter, and stretching from Alexander's conquest in 332 BCE to AD 641, is the Graeco-Roman Period.

Below: Mosaic of Alexander the Great defeating Darius, the Persian king, at the Battle of Issus. (*Jo St Mart*)

THE DIVINE KING

To understand the pharaoh's role in Egypt it is important to grasp his religious significance. As we have seen, it was believed that the pharaoh was descended from Horus. He was therefore semi-divine and would achieve full godhood after death. Falcon-headed Horus was the son of Osiris (the divine king) and Isis, conceived posthumously after Osiris had been murdered by his brother Seth and—somewhat gruesomely considering that Osiris' body had been dismembered—raised again to a semblance of life by his wife, Isis. Horus battled with his uncle for the return of his father's throne and upon his victory and accession an

Right: Pharaoh Ptolemy XII faces the gods Isis and Horus on this external wall of the famous Temple at Edfu. It is the second largest temple in Egypt, after Karnak. (*Jo St Mart*)

important part of his filial duty was the proper internment of Osiris' remains, an act mirrored in the ascension of all new pharaohs. As the spirit of Horus settled within the new king, so his predecessor (usually his father) was honored in a way befitting his new status as a full god merged with Osiris.

As the representative of the gods on Earth, the pharaoh drew his strength directly from them and was believed to be able to intercede with the divine on behalf of his people. In turn, the gods signaled their approbation of the pharaoh by blessing the River Nile with a flood that would bring a bountiful harvest or, if he incurred their displeasure, by withholding one. The latter was a serious matter, usually leading to a weakening of the pharaoh's power and, in one case (at the close of the Old Kingdom), in the total failure of the state.

Every sacrifice and offering was made in the pharaoh's name as the chief priest of all gods, and he was also responsible for upholding *maat* within his realm. Embodied by the beautiful daughter of the sun god (who can easily be identified by the feather of truth worn in her hair), *maat* is a difficult term to translate, but carries a sense of righteousness, of justice and order, and of unchanging continuity. *Maat* keeps chaos in abeyance. In this way, and guided by the spirit of Horus within, the pharaoh's role crossed over into the secular. He was expected to rule over legal matters as well as leading religious rites.

The king's divine status is symbolized by his regalia, which is familiar to us from Egyptian artworks and tomb carvings. The most important of these were the crook, which represents reward for innocence and kingship, and the flail with which the guilty were punished. The pharaoh also wore the dual crown of the two lands, Upper and Lower Egypt, which incorporated the Eye of Ra, or Ureaus Cobra, that watched over the pharaoh, protecting him and witnessing all he did.

Divinity was also conferred by the pharaoh's names.

Far left: This intricate frieze depicts Djehuti, also known as the Egyptian god Thoth. He was thought to represent the heart and tongue of Ra and as such became equated with writing, science, and arbitration. *(Jo St Mart)*

Left: This beautiful depiction of a sunrise appears on the coffin of Amenemope, the successor to Psusennes I. He had only a brief nine-year reign and was buried in Tanis alongside his father. *(Jo St Mart)*

Throughout history names have held great significance, but none more so than for the Ancient Egyptians. Dating from circa 2500 BCE, Egypt's king bore five names, only one of which was his birth name. Three of these reinforced the pharaoh's divine status and two his control over the two lands. The first was his Horus name, seen in relics within a rectangular *serekh* topped with the falcon god; the second was his *Nbty* or "Two Ladies" name, referring to Nekhbet and El-Kab, the two goddesses of Upper Egypt and Wadjet and Buto of Lower Egypt. In relics, the *Nbty* name can be identified as being prefixed by the vulture and cobra symbols of the goddesses of the two lands. The third of the king's names is known as the "Golden Horus," and again confirmed divinity, for gold was considered eternal. Indeed, it was believed that the gods' skin was golden. The *nisu-bity*, or "throne name," represented the dual mortal-divine aspects of the king and his lordship over the two lands. From the fourth dynasty onward it always included Ra (or Re), the name of the sun god. The king's final name was his birth name, and is the one by which we now identify the different pharaohs. It was generally preceded by an honorific, such as *Sa-re*, Son of Re.

While discussing names, it is appropriate to note that the word "pharaoh" would not have been used by Ancient Egyptians, at least not until relatively late. The term is a Hebrew adaptation of the Egyptian word "per-aa" (which translates as "great house"). Its first known use to describe the king dates to around 1450 BCE and is found in a letter written to Amenhotep IV. Before that, the word used to denote the king's title was *nisu*.

GOVERNMENT

In Ancient Egypt all power flowed from the pharaoh, yet a single man or woman could obviously not oversee every aspect of administration and there was a well-ordered system of government in place. Second to the pharaoh was the vizier, whose task it was to represent the king and maintain the country's bureaucracy in addition to coordinating construction projects, the legal system and land surveys, as well as overseeing archives and the treasury. Beneath the vizier were up to forty-two *nomarchs*, each responsible for a *nome*, or administrative district. Their job would have included collection of taxes, which were stored in temples. Minor legal disputes were settled by a local council of elders known as the *Kenbet* by the time of the New Kingdom, though the more serious would be fielded upward, often as far as the *Great Kenbet*, presided over by the vizier or the pharaoh himself. It is interesting to note that though penalties for serious crime were harsh, Ancient Egypt's legal system seems to have been geared toward common sense and reaching amicable agreement. In fact, to all appearances it was a remarkably progressive society for its time. Slaves excepted (and it is still not clear to what extent slaves were used, though it is now thought that the pyramids were raised by the general public rather than slaves pressed into service), all citizens were equal under the law. Although a rigid class system existed, with farmers at the bottom and nobles at the top, women were remarkably emancipated by the standards of the ancient world (and even by some modern standards), being able to hold land and participate in trade, petition the courts and the vizier, and marry and divorce at will.

Above farmers were craftsmen and artists whose work would have been sold in shops attached to the temple. while the upper class comprised scribes and officials. These were the so-called "white kilt" class, who showed their rank by wearing garments of bleached linen. Below only the nobility, the next highest rung on the social ladder was occupied by priests, physicians and—tellingly—engineers, an indication of how highly those with the skilled knowledge of erecting large structures were valued in Ancient Egyptian society.

As Egypt had no monetary system until the Late Period,

all commercial transactions were by barter. Taxes were levied on farm produce and cattle (usually after a harvest, but also at any time the pharaoh saw fit), while citizens were also expected to contribute their time to public works, under what is known as a *corvée* system. Although it is thought that it was possible for a subject to buy his way out of forced labor with higher payments of grain, the *corvée* system produced an enormous pool of free workers who were used to construct roads, irrigation channels, temples, and—of course—pyramids, as well as doing army service and mining.

In this way, the pharaoh exerted his control over every strata of society. Every citizen, from the lowest to the highest, in some way served the state, by paying heavy taxes or through forced labor or both. Those exempt—the priests for example—served the king more directly and drew their living from treasury funds. As the Nile Valley was fertile and rich in mineral wealth with a correspondingly large population that also enjoyed excellent trade links to the outside world, it is perhaps unsurprising that Egypt rose to prominence. The country's resources were enviable and largely concentrated in one pair of hands, those of the pharaoh.

Right: This tomb room was built for the vizier Mereruka, also known as Meri, who served under the pharaoh Teti. (*The Art Archive/Gianni Dagli Orti/AA390282*)

Section One
Predynastic and Early Dynastic Egypt
(Prehistoric–c. 2686 BCE)

The history of Egypt is closely associated with that of the River Nile. Indeed, it was the river that drew the earliest settlers to this verdant region in the late Paleolithic era, at which time the climate of northern Africa was becoming more hot and dry. In fact, it is believed that the Nile Valley was populated by hunter-gatherers some 1.8 million years ago, during the Pleistocene Period. Over time, these people became less nomadic and began to take advantage of the agricultural possibilities offered by the fertile floodplain. By about 5500 BCE tribes living along the banks of the Nile had evolved distinctive cultures, dependent on raising crops and animals, and had also developed advanced stone tools as well as artistic pottery and bronze metal work.

Notable among these peoples were a culture known as the Badari of southern Egypt, whose grave pits indicate that social hierarchies were being formed. Also in the south were a tribe known as the Naqada, whose advances include the manufacture of high quality jewelry from gold, ivory, and lapis lazuli, as well as decorated stone vases and

Left: This relief shows a triumphal procession of King Menes and is taken from the Narmer Palette which dates to c.3100 BCE.
(The Art Archive/Egyptian Museum Cairo/Alfredo Dagli Orti/AA325668)

Right: This ancient and worn stone is thought to be inscribed with the name of Djer who reigned Egypt for 57 years. (*Jo St Mart/British Museum*)

Above: The mark of Hor-Aha can be seen on this small tablet. The pharaoh's name, translated as "fighting hawk," is seen on many ancient labels and describes his reign as a difficult one. *(Jo St Mart/British Museum)*

Right: Reverse side of the Narmer Palette showing the pharaoh approaching ten decapitated enemies at the top. *(Jo St Mart)*

ceramics glazed with a compound known as faience.

To the north the Maadian folk left behind pottery that gives a tantalizing glimpse of the first stirrings of recognizable Egyptian culture. Among their relics archeologists have discovered pottery ornamented with serekhs that bear the first Horus names.

It is not until the Early Dynastic Period (c. 3150–2686 BCE) that the pharaohs rose to power. Some time at the beginning of this era the two lands of Upper and Lower Egypt became united and Egypt's history proper began. Little is known of the first rulers. The Greek-Egyptian historian Manetho suggests that the first king was Menes, though the first records indicate it was Hor-Aha. To add to the confusion, the first ruler to claim to have brought the two lands together is Narmer. In fact, it seems likely that Menes was entirely mythical or a mythicized Narmer, and that the unification of Egypt proceeded gradually rather than by conquest, with administration being centered on Memphis.

With bureaucracy came increased organization of agriculture, trade links, and wealth generation. At this time, in tandem with an increasingly sophisticated religious system, the rich began to build more impressive tombs. Known as mastabas, these were prototypes for the first step pyramids that were developed later. And as the worship of gods such as Horus, Seth, and Neith developed, so too did the notion of a king whose very nature was divine.

Narmer

c. 3150 BCE
0 Dynasty

There is much discussion pertaining to the true identity of Narmer and whether he can be regarded as the first pharaoh of Upper and Lower Egypt. Many believe he was the successor to Scorpion, the king of Upper Egypt in the Protodynastic Period. Others suggest that Narmer and Scorpion are one and the same, though no evidence exists to support that theory. The discovery of the Narmer Palette in 1898 (the oldest known Egyptian historical document) suggests that it was Narmer who unified the two states, as it shows him wearing the crowns of both Upper and Lower Egypt, making him the first king of what has been termed Dynasty 0, dated somewhere between 3150 to 3050 BCE. The almost perfectly preserved Narmer Palette is roughly 5,000 years old, and has been termed "the first historical document in the world." In fact, despite its beautiful carvings, the palette was probably a tool used in the manufacture of cosmetics.

Right: Attributed to King Scorpion, the Scorpion Mace Head was discovered in 1897 at Hierakonpolis. (*Jo St Mart*)

Hor-Aha

c. 3050 BCE
1st Dynasty

Hor-Aha is thought to be the first true pharaoh of the First Dynasty in Ancient Egypt, possibly having inherited the throne from his father, Narmer. Very few records remain concerning his reign though there is a legend surrounding the story of his death. It is told that he was taken away by Seth, the god of the desert, who while hunting had adopted the form of a hippopotamus. This tale led to some speculation that Hor-Aha was actually the legendary Menes—the Egyptian warrior who was allegedly the first man to be crowned king of both Upper and Lower Egypt, since both men died hunting hippopotamus. By the time of the Eighteenth Dynasty in Egypt, the tomb of Hor-Aha in Abydos had become an important part of religious ceremony since it was believed to be the true resting place of Osiris, the god of life and death.

Hor-Aha is also credited with founding the city of Memphis, just south of the Nile Delta. Positioned strategically between Upper and Lower Egypt, it would become one of the most important cities of ancient times.

Above: The Horus name of Hor-Aha appears on this potsherd at the British Museum. (*Jo St Mart/British Museum*)

Djer

c. 3040 BCE
1st Dynasty

Son of Hor-Aha and the second pharaoh of the 1st Dynasty, Djer is thought to have ruled for between forty-one and fifty-seven years. The clashing evidence over the length of his reign is found in the writings of the 3rd century BCE priest, Manetho, and on the Palermo Stone, a large stele inscribed with the Royal Annals of Ancient Egypt. Again, due to the scarcity of inscriptions relating to him, and the difficulty in translating what little we have, it is almost impossible to draw any firm conclusions about his reign. However, we do know the location of Djer's tomb at Abydos. It is surrounded by over 300 smaller burials, each of which is thought to have contained one of Djer's servants. As was traditional during that time, the pharaoh took all his retainers into the afterlife with him, though the practice was later abandoned, probably since it robbed the pharaoh's successor of useful and experienced staff. Instead, the pharaoh was buried with several "ushabtis," figurines who would carry out any tedious menial jobs on behalf of the king in the afterlife.

Below: The seal of the First Dyansty pharaoh, Djer, was discovered on this ancient carved stone. (*Jo St Mart/British Museum*)

Djet
c. 3008–3005 BCE
1st Dynasty

Unfortunately, no record of Djet's rule remains on the partially destroyed Palermo Stone, and much of what is known about him comes solely from his tomb in Abydos. He was buried with 172 of his vassals and a beautifully preserved funerary stele bearing Djet's Horus name (a title taken by the king to illustrate his worldly and holy power), "Horus Cobra." However, the carvings on the stele indicate that the unique Egyptian techniques and designs were becoming fully established by his reign. It is believed he was married to Queen Meritneith, who after her husband's early death, took over as regent for her young son, Den.

Right: Now located at the Louvre in Paris, this limestone stele depicts the serpent hieroglyph, the symbol for Djet, and a Horus falcon. It was discovered in tomb Z in Abydos. *(The Art Archive/Musée du Louvre Paris/Gianni Dagli Orti/AA371132)*

Den

c. 3005–2973 BCE
1st Dynasty

By the time of Den's reign, 1st Dynasty records become somewhat clearer. It is probable that Djet's successor ruled for over thirty-two years, while items found in his tomb attest to the king's martial prowess. Indeed, Den's Horus name was "Hor Den," meaning "Horus who strikes," and many of his funerary items depict a triumphant Den smiting his enemies. For example, a remarkable ivory label—now housed in the British Museum in London—shows him about to beat a kneeling captive chief. The battle depicted on the label seems to draw a parallel with a reference to the "Smiting of the Troglodytes" on the Palermo Stone. Den was succeeded by his son Anedjib, who ruled for approximately twenty-six years.

Above: A pot bearing the mark of the pharaoh Den. (*Jo St Mart/British Museum*)

Semerkhet

c. 2970–2955 BCE
1st Dynasty

With his name translating as "Thoughtful Friend," King Semerkhet ruled for somewhere between nine and eighteen years and is thought to have been plagued with political turmoil. The scribe Manetho attributes these to disputes caused by his succession, leading scholars to theorize that Semerkhet seized the throne from a rightful heir. Adding evidence to the hypothesis is the fact that, following Semerkhet's rise to power, the name of his predecessor, Anedjib, seems to have been obliterated from several important monuments. His tomb is in Abydos, in Upper Egypt, and is bigger than that of Anedjib, perhaps in another attempt to eclipse his rival. Although his name appears on the Palermo Stone, he is not listed on the Saqqara King List.

Right: This beautifully decorated ivory tablet was found in the tomb of pharaoh Semerkhet I and bears his name. (*Jo St Mart/British Museum*)

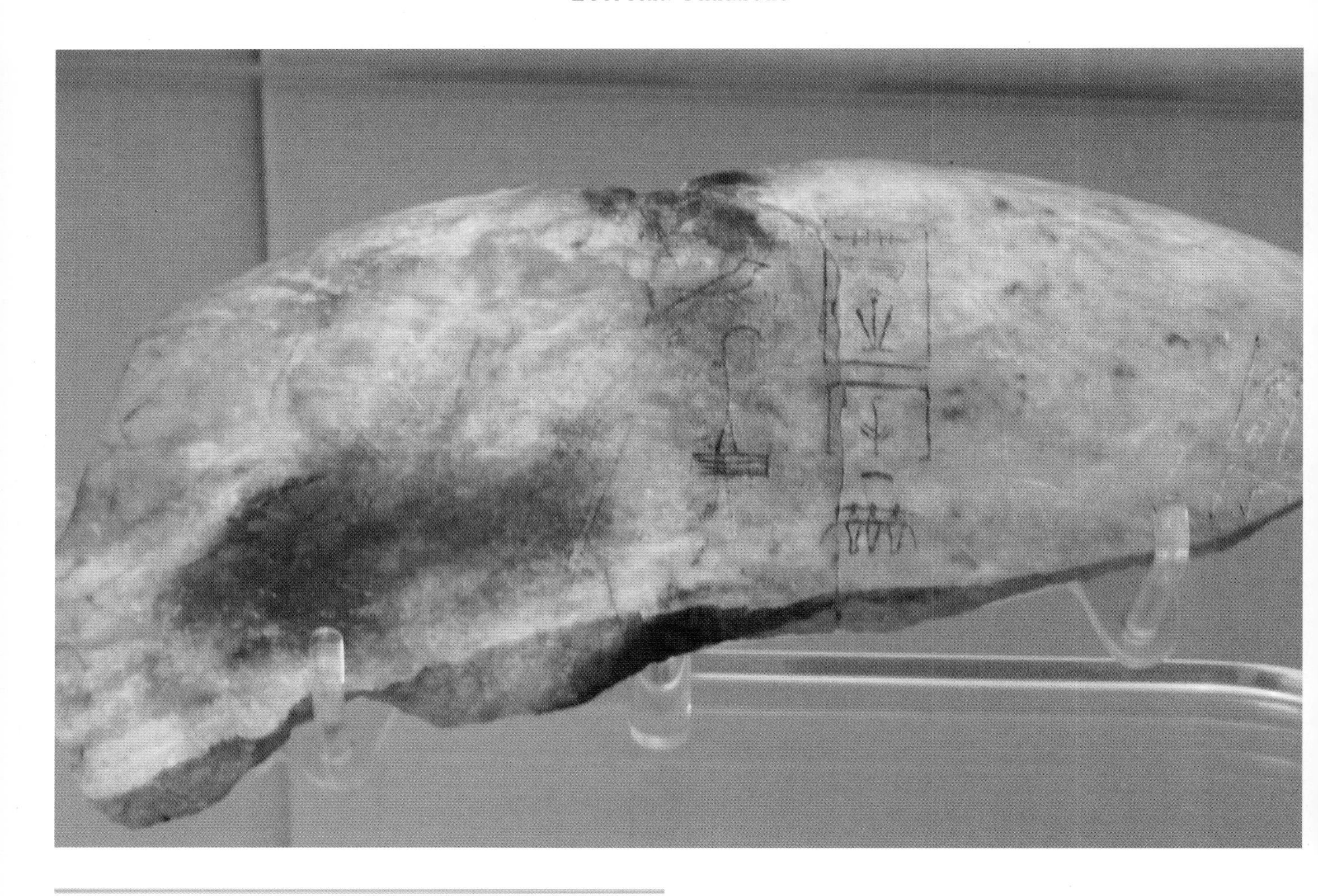

Qa'a

c. 2955–2929 BCE
1st Dynasty

The last king of the 1st Dynasty, Qa'a appears to have presided over a time of stability and bounty for the Egyptian people. He ruled for approximately twenty-six years before being succeeded by Hotepsekhemwy, the first pharaoh of the 2nd Dynasty. Beyond this, little remains to tell us of his reign. Located in Umm el-Qa'ab in Abydos, his tomb measures approximately thirty-three yards by twenty-five yards, and Qa'a was accompanied into the afterlife by twenty-six of his servants—perhaps one for each year of his sovereignty. Interestingly, the practice of sending retainers into the afterlife with the pharaoh seems to have petered out around this time.

Above: This tablet bears the mark of Qa'a, the last pharaoh of the first dynasty. His tomb was discovered in Abydos in 1993. *(Jo St Mart/British Museum)*

Hotepsekhemwy

c. 2890 BCE
2nd Dynasty

Extremely little is known regarding the first pharaoh of the 2nd Dynasty. Hotepsekhemwy, meaning "Pleasing in Powers," ruled for approximately thirty-eight years according to the writings of Manetho but, apart from a couple of seals bearing his name, little else dating to his time remains. Scholars do not believe him to have been the son of the previous pharaoh, Qa'a, but rather think he was the husband to the pharaoh's daughter. Relics that may have been from Hotepsekhemwy's tomb have been found in Saqqara, about twenty miles south of modern-day Cairo, but so far the pharaoh's final resting place has not been discovered and may have disintegrated completely.

Left: This small statue depicts a priest identified as Hotep-Dif at the base and dates to the reign of Hotepsekhemwy. (*Jo St Mart*)

Raneb

c. 2860 BCE
2nd Dynasty

Raneb, meaning "Re is the Lord," ruled for approximately thirty-nine years as far as scholars can tell and based on Manetho's list of kings. Once again there is very little information remaining that corroborates the exact time of his rule or any major events in his life. As with his successor, only a few relics that may have come from his tomb have been discovered at Saqqara. The tomb itself has not been found. Manetho does, however, relate that Raneb established religious cults whose members worshipped the holy goat of the city of Mendes and the sacred bull of Mnevis in Heliopolis.

Above: This Horus topped serrekh dates to the reign of Raneb and shows the pharaoh's name, which meant "Re is Lord." (*Jo St Mart*)

Section Two
The Old Kingdom
(c. 2686-2181 BCE)

Spanning over 500 years and four dynasties, the advent of the period now known as the Old Kingdom heralded a glorious golden age of Egyptian culture and an unprecedented surge in monument building. For this reason it is often also called "The Age of Pyramids."

By that time the idea that the pharaoh was of divine ancestry had firmly taken root and it was believed that it was his intercession that ensured the annual flood that was so important for Egyptian agriculture. With the pharaoh at their head, the Egyptians of the Old Kingdom began to think of themselves as "the only true human beings on Earth." It was also at the start of this period that Egypt was split into forty-two administrative *nomes*.

With an administrative system in place and a divine king at the head of the country, Ancient Egyptian culture as we know it today developed at an astonishing pace. More organized agriculture produced much higher yields, boosted yet further with the spread of irrigation systems, which helped provide the state with a surplus. This, together with the *corvée* system, which forced all citizens into labor on the king's behalf, provided a springboard for massive construction programs. Simultaneously, Egypt

Left: The second largest pyramid in Giza was Khafre's. It is believed that this impressive edifice was broken into and robbed as early as the First Intermediate Period. (*Jo St Mart*)

made technological and artistic strides that precipitated both an incredible level of engineering sophistication and fantastic works of sculpture, painting, jewelry, and literature.

Early in the 3rd Dynasty, the pharaoh Djoser (c. 2668–2649 BCE) commissioned the construction of a structure known as the step pyramid at Saqqara, the necropolis of Memphis. The first king of the 4th Dynasty, Snefru (c. 2613–2589 BCE), followed suit, ordering the construction of three pyramids, at Meidum (since collapsed), Dahshur (the Bent Pyramid), and the more modest Red Pyramid at North Dahshur. Snefru's son, Khufu

Above: This relief of Ptah, the god who called everything into being and is also the god of craftsmen, is thought to date back to the Late or Ptolemaic Dynasty. (*Jo St Mart*)

Right: Found in his *serdab*—a chamber within a pyramid complex set aside for statues of the dead—this limestone portrait is of Djoser. (*The Art Archive/Egyptian Museum Cairo/Gianni Dagli Orti/AA325788*)

(c. 2589–2566 BCE), raised perhaps the most famous building in history—the Great Pyramid at Giza—while Khufu's own sons, Djedfra (c. 2566–2558 BCE) and Khafra (c. 2558–2532 BCE), built a second pyramid next to it and the Sphinx as a monument to their father.

Their efforts were continued by their successors, but by the dawn of the 5th Dynasty, the extravagances of the pyramid builders were over. Building expenses had emptied the state's coffers, and the first king of the 5th Dynasty, Userkhaf (c. 2498–2491 BCE), further weakened the power of the pharaoh with reforms that led to his power being challenged by the regional *nomarchs* and eventually to civil war. The following centuries are characterized by increasing turmoil, and the Old Kingdom ended in turmoil after a dramatic drop in rainfall, beginning about 2200 BCE and lasting about fifty years, stopped the yearly flooding of the Nile. Bankrupt, riven by internal strife, and led by a pharaoh with whom the gods were evidently angry, Egypt descended into the chaos of the First Intermediate Period.

Below: Pepi II as a child sits on the lap of his mother Queen Ankhnesmerire. (*Jo St Mart*).

Djoser

c. 2668–2649 BCE
3rd Dynasty

Above: This massive statue depicts the pharaoh Djoser and is situated in the Cairo Egyptian Museum. (*Jo St Mart*)

The most famous of all the 3rd Dynasty kings, Djoser succeeded his brother to the throne and left Egypt one of its most celebrated monuments, the Step Pyramid at Saqqara. Very little is known about the actual rule of Djoser, but Egyptologists have pieced together enough evidence from various old shrines to divine the rough shape of his reign.

It seems that following the death of his brother, Djoser had to contend with much political upheaval, in spite of which he appears to have brought lands as far south as Aswan under his rule. He also sent out expeditions to the Sinai Peninsula to quell rising rebellion among the local inhabitants, and began the search for mineral deposits such as copper and turquoise. There has been much debate regarding the length of Djoser's reign. Manetho attributes Djoser with a rule of twenty-nine years, but according to the Turin King List, he ruled for only nineteen years. However, numerous scholars assert that nineteen years is far too short a time to complete the building projects that define Djoser's time in power, especially that of his tomb.

Undoubtedly one of the oldest remaining buildings in the world, Djoser's pyramid in Saqqara was probably the first structure to be completely made of stone and was the brainchild of one man: the vizier Imhotep, who was a man of many talents and richly honored by the pharaoh. It is likely that the pyramid began as a normal "mastaba" tomb—a flat-roofed, rectangular building usually made of mud bricks or stone—which was the standard type of the time, to which one mastaba after another was added as the pharaoh's ambitions soared, leaving earlier tombs boxed in. In order for the king to be placed in his burial chamber a new entrance was made from the north side and then shut with a three-ton cover of granite. Unfortunately, as is almost inevitable in the case of ancient and wealthy tombs, grave robbers have long since stolen Djoser's funerary treasures, but archaeologists have found many stone vases underneath the pyramid, all beautifully made. These are possibly examples of Imhotep's craftsmanship, since he is described elsewhere as a sculptor and vase maker. A painted limestone statue of Djoser was also discovered and is the oldest life-size Egyptian statue in the world. A mummified left foot discovered in one of the inner corridors, however, is possibly all that remains of the pharaoh's body.

Sekhemkhet

c. 2649–2643 BCE
3rd Dynasty

King Sekhemkhet is thought to have been pharaoh for just six years. Almost nothing was known of him before 1951, when Zakaria Goneim found the remains of an incomplete pyramid close to Djoser's step pyramid at Saqqara. While surveying the land, Goneim noticed an unusual terrace close to the southwestern side of the Djoser enclosure. Noting that there was a great deal of building rubble around it, Goneim concluded the site must contain something more interesting. Over the following months the archeologist cleared the area and to his surprise discovered what appeared to be the beginnings of a gigantic step pyramid. Although it had not been completed it would have reached a height of 230 feet, some 16 feet taller than Djoser's pyramid. It is presumed that the huge structure was unfinished because of the suddenness of Sekhamkhet's demise.

Goneim later uncovered a hidden entrance leading down to a passageway. Here he found several items

Below: This ivory plaque was found in the tomb of Sekhemkhet. *(The Art Archive/Egyptian Museum Cairo/Gianni Dagli Orti/AA393431)*

Above: The successor to Djoser, King Sekhemhet, never completed his great funerary pyramid at Saqqarah and now only the half buried doorway remains.
(*The Art Archive/Gianni Dagli Orti/AA421320*)

including golden jewelry and exquisite trinkets that seemed not to have been disturbed by robbers. Once inside the complex, and after a concentrated effort to clear dangerous rubble, Goneim eventually discovered the burial chamber itself. The name of Sekhemkhet was found on seals within the hall and on a large, alabaster sarcophagus inside. Like the rest of the tomb, it was intact and undisturbed, but strangely, when the team of archeologists opened Sekhemkhet's coffin, it was empty.

Huni

c. 2637–2613 BCE
3rd Dynasty

The last king of the 3rd Dynasty, Huni accomplished several important goals during his twenty-four-year reign, including the construction of a stronghold—as well as a small ceremonial pyramid—on the island of Elephantine, which protected the country's southern border along the Nile near Aswan. It is also speculated that he was responsible for the great stepped pyramid at Meidum, though Huni appears to have died before it was completed (it was later finished by Snefru) and may have been buried subsequently in the Meidum necropolis. Among his consorts was Meresankh who bore him his successor, Snefru, while evidence also suggests that he fathered Hetepheres, his son's future wife and therefore his half-sister.

Right: A red granite carving thought to be of the pharaoh Huni. (*Jo St Mart*)

Below: The ruins of Aswan. (*The Art Archive/Gianni Dagli Orti/AA391770*)

Snefru

c. 2613–2589 BCE
4th Dynasty

Heralding the foundation of the 4th Dynasty, the reign of Snefru, meaning "he who perfects," was a golden era for Egypt, and it appears that he was considered by his people to be a fair and judicious king. Under Snefru's guidance Egypt began to step up trade with neighboring countries. Indeed, an inscription on the Palermo Stone tells of Snefru sending forty great ships to the Lebanon to fetch giant logs of cedar, and also ordering trips to Sinai for turquoise. These would have been essential raw materials for the construction of temples and ships. It seems that Snefru kept close ties with Sinai; in fact, evidence found there suggests that he was worshipped as a god in that region.

He was also a keen builder, and though his son Khufu has been credited as the most prolific builder of pyramids, it is actually Snefru who should be awarded this title. During his lifetime he completed three: the Huni Pyramid at Meidum, the Bent Pyramid at Dahshur, named for its strange asymmetrical shape, and the Red Pyramid at the Dahshur necropolis.

Left: A view of the corbelled vault inside the Red Pyramid of Snefru, the king of the Fourth Dynasty, situated at Dahshur. (*The Art Archive/Gianni Dagli Orti/AA390845*)

Far left: The famous "Bent Pyramid" of the pharaoh Snefru located at the royal necropolis in Dahshur. The old Egyptian name for the tomb is "Snefru shining in the South." (*The Art Archive/Gianni Dagli Orti/AA390846*)

Khufu

c. 2589–2566 BCE
4th Dynasty

It is believed that Khufu took control of the throne when he was in his twenties and ruled for approximately twenty-three years. Unlike his father, it is probable that he was a cruel and merciless leader. He is, however, credited as the force behind the construction of the Great Pyramid at Giza, the only remaining one of the original Seven Wonders of the Ancient World and still the most instantly recognizable building on Earth.

During his reign Khufu continued his father's policy of maintaining a military presence in the Sinai Peninsula, with the purpose of subduing the local populace and retaining control of the turquoise mines. He is also thought to have quarried the red granite of the Aswan area. It seems, though, that his ruling passion was the building of his monument and it is for the Great Pyramid that he is now principally known.

Right: This ancient stone, found near his tomb, bears the Horus name of the pharaoh Khufu. (*Jo St Mart/British Museum*)

Below: The Solar boat of Khufu measures 143ft. (*Jo St Mart*)

The first of the pharaohs to break away from the traditional burial grounds at Saqqara or Dahshur, Khufu chose instead the Giza plateau and concentrated all his energy on the completion of his great monument. In fact, several stories illustrate just how far the king was willing to go in order to ensure his dream came to fruition. One apocryphal example relates how Khufu put one of his daughters into prostitution in order to make money for the cost of construction. The story goes that, as well as the fee for her services, she also demanded each client provide her with a large brick. In this way she not only assisted her father with the building of his pyramid, but was also able to acquire the materials necessary for her own tomb.

It is thought that Khufu's pyramid took about twenty years to build and to this day experts are unsure how the construction was completed. It was originally 481 feet high and each side measures almost exactly (give or take eight inches at the most) 755 feet and comprises approximately 2,300,000 separate blocks, each weighing about 2.20 tons. (The larger, heavier blocks are estimated to weigh 15 tons.) The outside of the pyramid was once enclosed in white Tura limestone, which would have reflected the sunlight, although unfortunately most of it was stolen and used to build Cairo during the Middle Ages. The grand mortuary temple, situated on the eastern side of the pyramid was also pillaged and all that remains of this once impressive structure is the black basalt floor.

Surrounding the pyramid are the tombs of Khufu's many servants, who were to accompany the king on his journey to the next life, where they would continue their lives of servitude to the king.

Archeologists also discovered the lavishly decorated tomb of Khufu's mother, Queen Hetep-Heres, close to the southern face of his pyramid and, most surprisingly, in 1954 archaeologists uncovered a completely intact wooden ship. Carefully restored over many years, this has been displayed in a specifically designed museum since 1982.

The interior of Khufu's final resting place is as impressive as its dimensions imply. The Grand Gallery with its 28-foot-high ceilings leads up to the King's Chamber in the center of the pyramid. It is in this room that the huge sarcophagus was discovered. Too large to have fitted through any of the doors, it was carved from a single block of Aswan granite and probably lowered into the chamber before the roof was added. The roof itself was completed with the placement of nine 45-ton granite blocks.

Strangely, considering the magnificence of his tomb, thus far only one tiny depiction of the king has been discovered, in 1903 by Flinders Petrie at the temple of Osiris in Abydos. However, from inscriptions we know that he fathered, nine sons and fifteen daughters. Very little is known of his wives, though among them was Meritates, thought to be his half-sister and mother of his successor, Djedefre.

Below: The Great Pyramid of Khufu. *(Jo St Mart)*

Djedefre

c. 2566–2558 BCE
4th Dynasty

Ruling for just nine years, Djedefre was the first pharaoh to take the name "Son of Ra" as his Horus name, perhaps demonstrating the increased regard given to the followers of the Sun God, Ra. Beyond this not a great deal is known of his relatively short eight- or nine-year rule. He was married to Hetepheres II, his half-sister and the widow of his brother Kawab, though it is possible that this marriage took place merely as a mutually beneficial arrangement that allowed Hetepheres II to retain her position at court despite the loss of her husband, and Djedfre to secure his place as ruler by marrying an heir of Khufu. This would have been especially useful if he was the offspring of a lesser wife, rather than the Khufu's chief queen.

Above: This red quartzite bust is of Djedfre and now resides at the Louvre. (*The Art Archive/Musée du Louvre/Gianni Dagli Orti/AA390206*)

Khafre

2558–2532 BCE
4th Dynasty

The fourth ruler of the 4th Dynasty, Khafre was another son of the prolific King Khufu and seems to have followed his father's example in numerous ways. He appears to have been a harsh and unforgiving monarch and the people of Egypt suffered under his (approximately) twenty-six-year rule. (Manetho sites his rule as lasting sixty-six years, but this cannot be corroborated.) By far the most famous accomplishment of Khafre's reign was the addition of another massive funerary complex by his father's pyramid at Giza, a complex that the Egyptian people must have endured great hardships to build.

Khafre's tomb at Giza would set the benchmark for later kings of the Old Kingdom. Not satisfied with just a pyramid, Khafre also built a valley temple and a causeway leading to a mortuary temple, not to mention the Sphinx. The valley temple is now one of the few large buildings dating back to the Old Kingdom that remains standing, though it has lost its roof. The pyramid—though smaller than that of his father—appears larger because Khafre had it built on slightly higher ground. In fact, even after the Great Pyramid lost thirty feet from its tip, it is still three feet taller than Khafre's tomb.

The tomb was once believed to be completely solid, but the Italian architect Giovanni Belzoni discovered the entrances into the pyramid in 1818 and, on entering, found a central burial chamber that had unfortunately already been scavenged by grave robbers. All that remained inside was a sarcophagus made of red granite containing a few animal bones.

The Great Sphinx, with its half-human, half-lion appearance, is one of the world's oldest statues. If, as it is generally believed, it is a representation of King Khafre, then it is also the oldest surviving royal portrait. Standing at 241 feet in length and 65 feet high, it was carved from local limestone and represents Re-Harakhte, the Sun God. Scholars believe it was built between 2520 BCE and 2494 BCE, thus firmly placing its construction within Khafre's reign. Although several theorists have suggested the Sphinx pre-dates all the monuments in Giza by thousands of years, there is little evidence to back these ideas. Khafre died before the completion of his great tomb, and the work was completed by his son and successor, Menkaure.

Below: This diorite statue of Khafre shows the famous builder of the second pyramid at Giza wearing the nemes head cloth and beard of the pharaoh with Horus behind. (*Art Archive/Egyptian Museum Cairo/ Alfredo Dagli Orti/AA325692*)

Menkaure

c. 2532–2504 BCE
4th Dynasty

Compared to his father and grandfather, Menkaure was a wise and gentle ruler. Although most now believe he ruled Egypt for roughly twenty-eight years, an interesting legend surrounding Menkaure implies his reign was much shorter. According to the tale, the gods were angered by the benevolence of Menkaure's rule and in a fit of righteous anger they sent word through the oracle at Buto that the king would be allowed to rule for only six years, and then the torment of Egypt would begin again. Knowing that his rule could end only by his demise, Menkaure decreed that candles should be kept alight during the night, thus fooling the gods into thinking it was daytime. In this way he hoped to lengthen his reign to twelve years. Unfortunately for Menkaure, the gods were not so easily tricked and on the sixth year of his reign, according to the legend, Menkaure died. It is a fantastic, yet nevertheless completely untrue, tale.

Menkaure was responsible for the construction of the final and smallest pyramid at Giza. Less than half the height of Great Pyramid of Khufu, it reaches just 228 feet. Nobody is quite sure why Menkaufe chose such a diminutive tomb, but it seems likely that after the effort of building his father's and grandfather's great monuments, the country would have been financially suffering and the work force exhausted.

Far left: Visitors flock to see the pyramids and Sphinx. (*Jo St Mart*)

Left: The pyramid of Menkaure, the third to be built at Giza, was originally encased in red granite at its base but its higher levels were covered in white Tura limestone, making it the first multi-colored pyramid. (*Jo St Mart*)

Above left: Slate dyad statue of Menkaure and his wife. (*Jo St Mart*)

Shepseskaf

c. 2504–2500 BCE
4th Dynasty

The second son of King Menkaure took the throne for just four years and his reign signified the end of the 4th Dynasty. Shepseskaf was handed power following the death of his father and the untimely death of his older brother, Prince Khuenre. Shepseskaf means "his soul is noble." It is thought he was the son of one of the lesser queens of Menkaure. Following the huge undertakings of the pyramids on the Giza Plateau, Shepseskaf chose to build his tomb at the 3rd Dynasty burial ground at Saqqara. Called "Mastaba el-Faraoun," meaning "pharaoh's bench," it is shaped like a large sarcophagus. Unfortunately, it has not weathered the ages well and very little remains. His half-sister, Princess Khentkawes, went on to marry the first king of the 5th Dynasty, Userkaf.

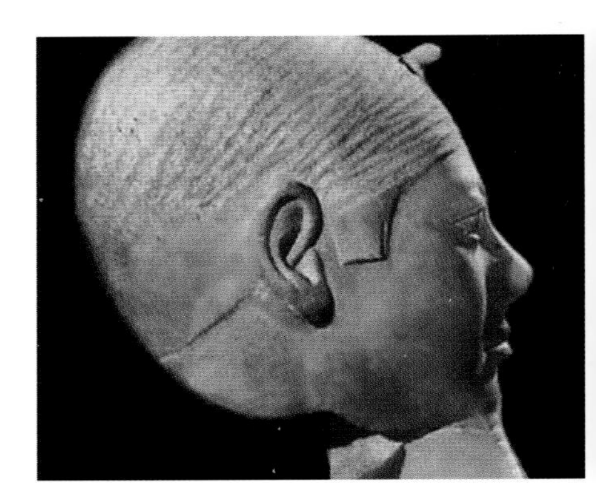

Right: While it has been suggested that this alabaster head may be of Menkaure it is generally believed to depict Shepseskaf. (*Jo St Mart*)

Userkaf

c. 2498–2491 BCE
5th Dynasty

Above: This is all that remains of the once great pyramid of pharaoh Userkaf in Saqqara. The exterior is in complete ruin and this has left the interior unreachable. (*Jo St Mart*)

The first king of the new dynasty, Userkaf was a descendant of Djedefre—his grandson to be precise. By marrying Princess Khentkawes, the half-sister of Menkaure, he cemented his claim to the throne. Userkaf decided to move away from the colossal buildings on the Giza Plateau and chose instead to build his tomb in Saqqara, near the original site of Djoser's great funerary monument, and was the first of the pharaohs to place his pyramid in a south-facing position. An apparently devout follower of the sun god, Userkaf would have chosen the spot specifically because it guaranteed that the rays of the sun would touch the tomb throughout the day. In fact, because of their zeal for this cult, he and his descendents were often referred to as "the Sun Kings." Userkaf would also go on to build a sun temple at Abu-Gurob. This massive limestone-and-mud brick podium and obelisk stood behind a raised sun altar.

Sahure

c. 2491–2477 BCE
5th Dynasty

Much of what is known about Sahure has been discovered through the writings of the Palermo Stone and from the remains of his tomb in Abusir, near the ancient burial grounds of Saqqara. He was the second king of the 5th Dynasty and most likely one of the sons of Userkaf and Queen Khentkawes I. There is no evidence that he had any wives or children, and was succeeded by his brother, Neferirkare.

Egypt saw very little conflict under the reign of Sahure, who seemed to prefer expansion through economic interactions. In fact, several of the remarkably preserved reliefs inside his pyramid document the many expeditions the pharaoh sent to foreign lands in order to trade. There are depictions of great Egyptian ships bringing back cedar from the Lebanon and Sahure also oversaw the first trip to the bountiful land of Punt. His emissaries brought back large quantities of myrrh, malachite, and electrum. Due to the many seafaring voyages undertaken during Sahure's reign, he is often considered the original founder Egypt's mighty naval force.

Left: This small dyad statue of the pharaoh Sahure shows him sitting next to a smaller man. (*Jo St Mart*)

Below: This relief from the funerary temple of Sahure depicts gods of plant shoots, fertility, and water. (*Art Archive/Egyptian Museum Cairo/Gianni Dagli Orti/AA390762*)

Neferirkare Kakai

c. 2477–2467 BCE
5th Dynasty

According to the list of kings compiled by Manetho, Neferirkare ruled for twenty years, but the writings of the Palermo Stone and the unfinished condition of his pyramid would seem to imply his reign was much shorter. In fact, scholars believe it was closer to ten years. His tomb at Abusir, if completed, would have been impressive, but only the main pyramid and the lower mortuary temple were finished. The size of the king's tomb suggests he was an eminent ruler, but very little else is known about his reign, though it is thought that he was a benign king.

Above: This piece of scroll is thought to date back to the reign of Neferirkare Kakai. (*Musée du Louvre, Paris*)

Below: South of the Solar Temple of Abu-Gurob lie the now ruined pyramids of Neferirkare, Niuserre, and Sahure. (*Jo St Mart*)

Niuserre Ini

c. 2453–2422 BCE
5th Dynasty

There is some debate as to the length and time of Niuserre Ini's reign. Manetho attributes this king with a rule of forty-four years, but many Egyptologists disagree, putting his reign somewhere between ten and thirty years. He is believed to be the son of Neferirkare Kakai and Queen Khentkawes II, and was married to Reptynub, though nothing else is known about this woman. Like his immediate forebears, he built a great solar temple at Abusir, which is the largest and best preserved in all of Egypt. It was the first and only temple to be built completely from stone and includes many pictographs, the most famous being the creation of the world by the sun god, Re. There are also drawings of the Festival of Sed and the changing seasons all over Egypt. The lavishness of the temple would suggest that the cult of Re had become extremely popular by this time.

Below left: Detail showing the pyramid of Niuserre at the necropolis of Abusir. (*The Art Archive/Gianni Dagli Orti/AA393893*)

Below: A statue of Niuserre which was found in his pyramid, itself the best preserved of the complexes at Abusir. (*Brooklyn Museum*)

Djedkare Isesi

c. 2414–2375 BCE
5th Dynasty

With his name meaning "the Soul of Re Endures," Djedkare Isesi ruled for approximately thirty-eight years. He was the first king of the 5th Dynasty, and broke with tradition by not building a solar temple at Abusir, preferring to build his pyramid in Saqqara. Scholars think this was the first sign that the cult of the sun god was waning in power, soon to be replaced by the followers of Osiris.

Above: Doorway to the tomb of Djedkare Isesi (*Jo St Mart*)

Right: This stele was discovered in an alleyway outside the tomb of king Unas in Saqqara. (*The Art Archive/Gianni Dagli Orti/AA360826*)

Unas

c. 2375–2345 BCE
5th Dynasty

The last king of the 5th Dynasty, Unas was married to Queens Khenut and Nebit. Although he left no sons, he did have at least one daughter, Iput. She would go on to marry Teti I, who would succeed Unas to the throne.

The discovery of Unas' pyramid at Saqqara in 1881 revealed several interesting facts. As well as reliefs documenting the major events of his reign, including the details of a famine, bargaining with foreign powers, and

tales of great hunts that he took part in, Unas was also the first of the pharaohs to have "spells" inscribed on the interior walls of his tomb. These were added to help the king cross over into the afterlife and guide him to the right-hand side of the sun god, Re. This practice soon became the norm for all future pharaohs of the next dynasty.

Also within this mortuary complex were two enormous boat pits, though it is unclear whether they ever actually held boats or were simply representational of the journey Unas would make while sailing with Re across the sky. The pyramid of Unas is also unique in that its exterior façade was restored by a high priest of the 19th Dynasty named Khaemwaset, with an inscription on the south side of the pyramid describing what had been done. Unfortunately the inscription did not withstand the passing of time and collapsed onto the desert floor. It was restored and put back in its original place in 1940.

Below: A detailed view of the cartouche of Unas, which was found in the entrance to his tomb in Saqqara. (*The Art Archive/Gianni Dagli Orti/AA391811*)

Teti

c. 2345–2333 BCE
6th Dynasty

Teti took the throne after a period of political upheaval following the death of Unas, marrying the former pharaoh's daughter Iput in order to consolidate his claim. He adopted the Horus name "Seheteptawy," which means "He who makes peace in the Two Lands," and this implies that there was strife between Upper and Lower Egypt at the time. Studies of his reign put its length at around twelve years, during which Teti is believed to have continued trading with Nubia and Babylos. He also seems to have tried to curry favor with his own, increasingly powerful, court officials and noblemen. In fact, the burial sites of many members of court are so lavish that they compare favorably with those of previous pharaohs. The huge tomb of Teti's chancellor alone contained thirty-two intricately carved rooms. This transference of wealth from the king to the bureaucrats would signal the end of the Old Kingdom, and Manetho writes that Teti was murdered by some of his own personal guards in a harem plot, though this has never been corroborated. His body was interred in the royal necropolis at Saqqara.

Above: Painted relief of the pharaoh Teti who is thought to have been assassinated by his own guard. (*Jo St Mart*)

Left: The ruined remains of Teti's pyramid. The burial chamber contained a simple coffin of wood when it was discovered. (*Jo St Mart*)

Pepi I

2332–2283 BCE
6th Dynasty

Although Pepi I was the rightful heir to the throne, it is believed that a man named Userkare briefly seized control shortly after the death of Pepi's father, Teti. Theorists suggest that it was Userkare, who planned the murder of Teti, and that the assassination may have been linked to the pharaoh's abandonment of the cult of Re. However, if true, the usurper does not seem to have held onto the throne for long and would have been ousted by Pepi I, almost certainly assisted by the powerful nobles at court. Their support would have come at a cost, however, and could be a contributing factor in further weakening the pharaoh's grip on Egypt, and thus ensuring the downfall of the Old Kingdom.

It is thought that Pepi, like his father, maintained close political and commercial ties with Babylos and continued expanding his territory into Nubia. Pepi was dedicated to the construction of monuments and during his long reign of roughly fifty years he commissioned buildings at Dendera, Abydos, the Isle of Elephantine, and Hierakonpolis, as well as a great canal at the First Cataract.

His first wife, Weret-Yamtes, was accused of conspiring against the king, and then disappears from all records. His following wives fared better. He married the two daughters of the high-ranking nobleman Khui of Abydos and made his son, Djau, the court vizier. It is not known exactly how many times the king married but so far archaeologists have unearthed six queens' pyramids close to the final resting place of Pepi I. His mortuary complex is called "Mennefer Pepy," and through the ages this transformed into the name "Memphis."

Right: The pharaoh Pepi I is seen in this kneeling statue holding a pair of small vases, an offering to a god. (*Jo St Mart*)

Merenre Nemtyemsaf I

c. 2283–2278 BCE
6th Dynasty

The son of King Pepi I and Queen Ankhesenpepi I, Merenre was the fourth ruler of the 6th Dynasty. It was originally thought that Merenre took the role of co-regent with his father before becoming the rightful king, but scholars studying the South Saqqara Stone—the inscribed lid of Queen Ankhesenpepi's sarcophagus, which lists the 6th Dynasty pharaohs—suggest that Merenre succeeded his father immediately after the latter's death and ruled for approximately twelve years. Little else is documented save that Merenre continued his father's expansion into Nubia and appointed Weni the Elder as the first governor of Upper Egypt.

Below: A mummy thought to be that of Merenre who enjoyed only a brief reign before his brother Pepi II came to the throne. (*Jo St Mart*)

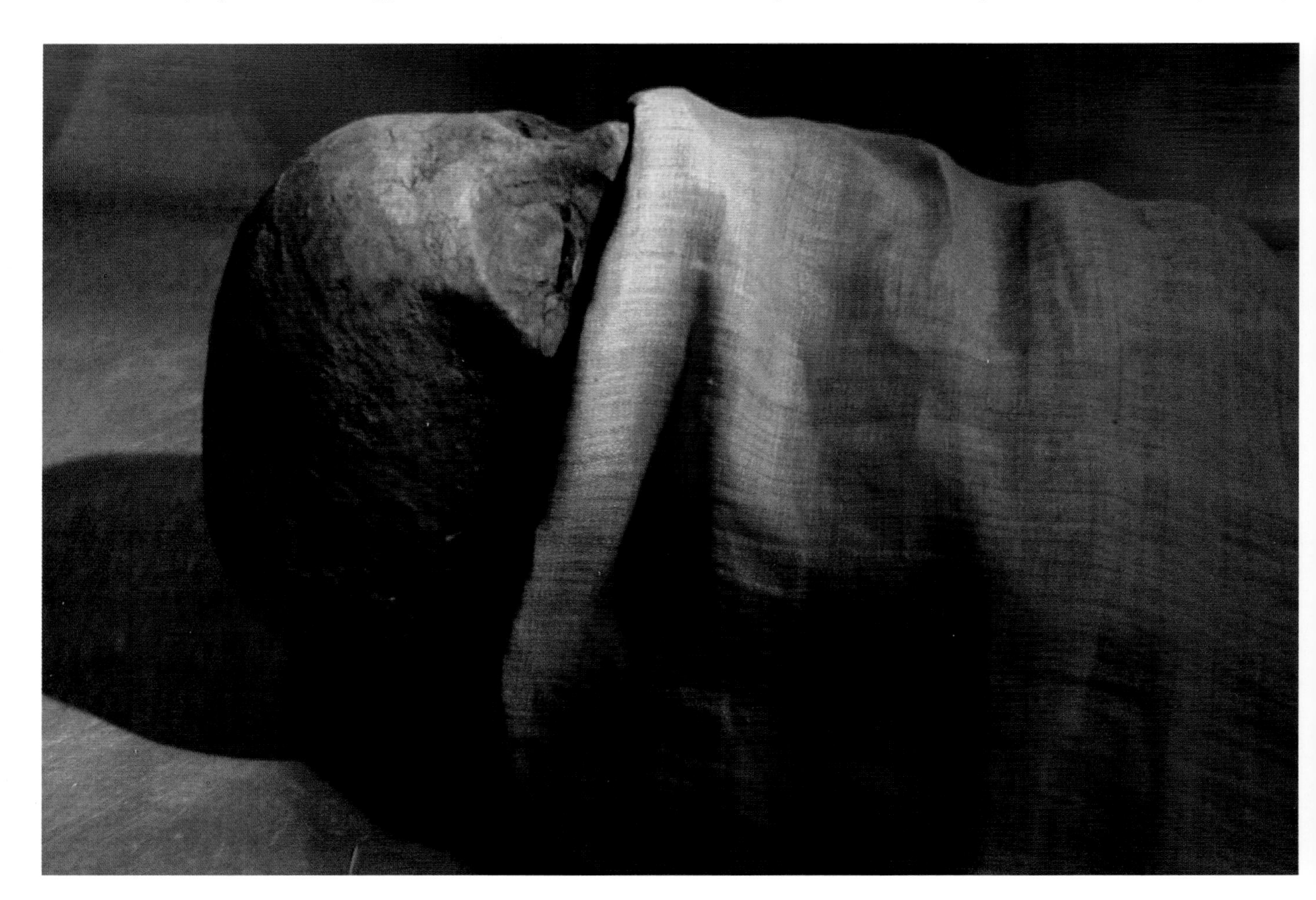

Pepi II

2278 BCE – 2184 BCE
6th Dynasty

Despite his presiding over the collapse of the Old Kingdom, King Pepi II's is recognized as the longest reign of any ruler in history, having apparently spanned an incredible ninety-four years (though some Egyptologists suggest the more realistic sixty-four). Historians once thought that he was the younger brother of the previous king, Menenre, but recent studies of the South Saqqara Stone revealed that he was, in fact, his son who would have been about six years old when he was crowned pharaoh. During Pepi II's reign the power of the nomarchs, or governors, grew stronger and the power of the pharaoh slowly disappeared. Shortly after the death of Pepi II the Old Kingdom ended as the local nobles fell into in-fighting and territorial disputes.

Left: It is thought that Pepi II would have been eight years old when this alabaster statuette showing him on his mother's knee was carved for the tomb of an Egyptian noble. (*Jo St Mart*)

Below: The pyramid of Pepi II who is thought to have been Egypt's longest ruler is now a mound of rubble at Saqqara. (*Jo St Mart*)

SECTION THREE
The First Intermediate Period
(c. 2181–2060 BCE)

As might be expected of a time so distant from our own, and from which few records have survived, historians disagree on the dates at which the Old Kingdom can be said to have broken down, heralding the era of political turmoil known as the First Intermediate Period. However, many consider the Old Kingdom to have ended with the 1st Dynasty and the First Intermediate Period to have encompassed the 7th, 8th, 9th, and 10th Dynasties, as well as part of the 11th. What is more certain is that during this period there were disruptions to peace in Egypt and the land was plagued by famine. The tomb of one king—Ankhtifi, who ruled during the early First Intermediate Period—bears inscriptions that detail the miserable state of the country. Other writings suggest a breakdown of rule and invasion by foreign armies. Taxation was high and the annual flood of the Nile either did not arrive or was unusually low, leading to widespread famine. It seems likely that this was an era of grave robbery, when most of the fabulous wealth that accompanied nobles to their tombs was stolen.

Left: This relief slab of Kheti dates to the beginning of 12th Dynasty. Kheti was the ruler of Heracleopolis in the First Intermediate Period. (*Jo St Mart*)

Against this backdrop of starvation and misery, Egypt fragmented, and local wars became endemic. Once people were released from their onerous duties to the pharaoh, however, parts of Egypt began to recover. Archeological evidence points to increasingly elaborate funerals across every class in the provinces, which suggests that wealth formerly taken in taxes now remained with those who earned it, and as the First Intermediate Period progressed there appears to have been an upsurge in artistic and literary endeavor in pockets along the Nile.

About 2160 BCE a new line of pharaohs (the 9th and 10th Dynasties) was founded by the descendants of the pharaoh Akhtoy. From their seat of power in Herakleopolis Magna they gradually brought all of Lower Egypt under their rule. Meanwhile, to the south in Upper Egypt, the Intef family (the 11th Dynasty) consolidated their own power at Thebes and slowly began expanding their lands northward. War was inevitable, and about 2060 BCE the pharaoh of Lower Egypt was defeated by Mentuhotep I. The Two Lands were finally reunited under a single pharaoh and the 11th Dynasty ushered in a new era of prosperity and cultural growth that is now known as the Middle Kingdom.

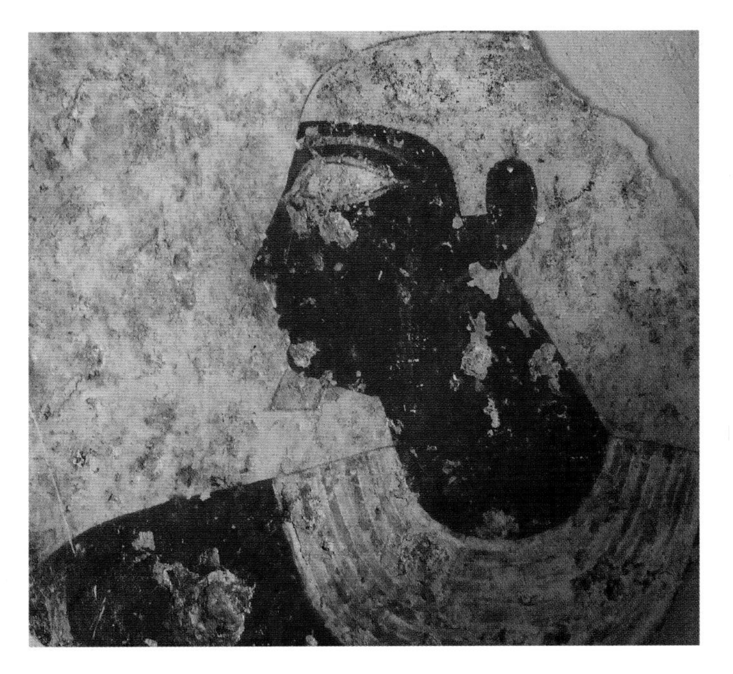

Above: The sarcophagus lid of Qakare Iby, from the short-lived Eighth Dynasty was discovered in a surprisingly small tomb. Little is known about this elusive pharaoh. (*Egyptian Museum of Torino Italy*)

Left: Detail from a painting inside the tomb of Qakare Iby. (*Egyptian Tourist Board*)

Left: It is thought that Nikare commissioned this statue of himself, his wife and his daughter for his funerary temple at Saqqara. The differences in size reflect their importance. (*Jo St Mart*)

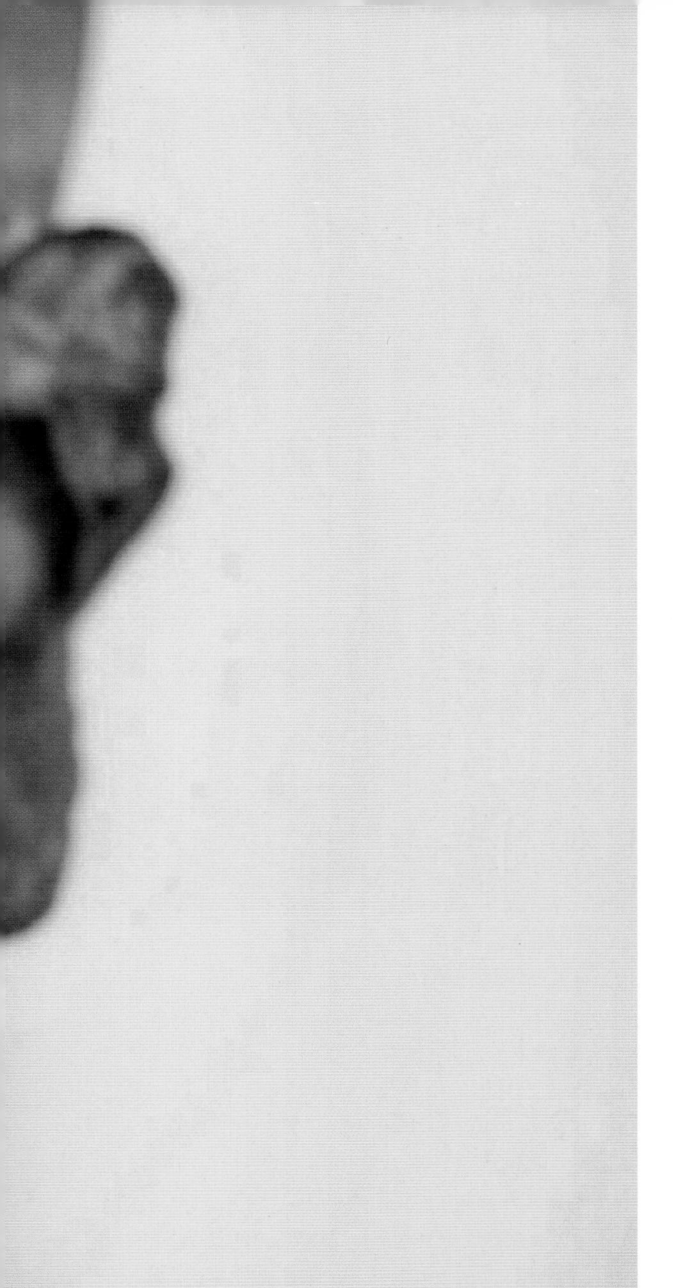

Section Four
The Middle Kingdom
(c. 2060–1782 BCE)

Encompassing the latter part of the 11th Dynasty up to the 14th Dynasty, the era now known as the Middle Kingdom witnessed a resurgence in building works and Egyptian culture generally. With the country reunified under the rule of Mentuhotep I, stability returned, though it was not until the 12th Dynasty that Egypt could be said to have returned to its former glories.

When the last pharaoh of the 11th Dynasty (Mentuhotep III) died childless, there seems to have been a bloodless transition of power to his former vizier, Amenemhet, who became Amenemhet I, founder of the 12th Dynasty. Under him, a new capital was constructed and named Itjtawy (at a location that is uncertain but thought to be at modern-day el-Lisht). Lingering small-scale civil strife was dealt with by force, and the pharaoh also curbed the powers of the provincial *nomarchs*, consolidating his own. As the 12th Dynasty progressed fresh irrigation works commenced, campaigns were launched against mineral-rich former Egyptian lands in Nubia that had been lost during the First Intermediate Period, and a massive construction campaign commenced on "The Walls of the Ruler" along the eastern Nile Delta, providing additional defense from foreign invasion.

Left: The more human features of this black granite statue of Amenemhet III contrast sharply with the more generic images of previous pharaohs. *(Jo St Mart)*

Above: This carving dates to the early reign of Mentuhotep II who initiated numerous construction projects despite his relatively short reign. (*Jo St Mart*)

Trade links improved and fresh mining and quarrying works opened throughout Egyptian territories. Stability and plenty provided the foundation for a wealth of achievements in literature, art, and construction, notably of a fabulous temple—now destroyed—at Abydos. Amenemhet I also pioneered a new development by naming his son Senusret (Senusret I, 1971–1926 BCE) as co-regent, albeit with junior status. This move provided the successor with valuable experience in wielding power, and ensured that when Amenemhet I was murdered, his son was able to quell a coup. Thereafter, co-regency was commonplace during the 12th Dynasty.

Amenemhet III (1842–1797 BCE) would, however, be the last of the great kings of the Middle Kingdom. During his reign, the cost of construction projects had again stripped the royal purse and Egypt's population had risen beyond the capacity of its agriculture to feed them. Amenemhet III brought Asiatic settlers to the delta region to work on construction (a decision that would later prove to be part of the Middle Kingdom's undoing), but it seemed that the gods were displeased once more and the Nile floods began to fail.

After a further two brief reigns—those of Amenemhet IV (1798–1786 BCE) and his sister Sobeknefru (1785–1782 BCE)—the dynasty ran out of heirs and a weakened Egypt was left to the relatively short-lived 13th and 14th Dynasties, whose control slipped as that of the Asiatic settlers in the delta region grew. Known as the Hyskos ("desert princes"), these settlers seized power of the north in circa 1720 BCE, and during the following years Egypt once more fell into fragmented confusion.

Above: Statue of Amenemhet II whose comparitively proserous reign lasted roughly thirty-four years. (*Jo St Mart*)

Left: Now at the Museum of Fine Arts in Boston, this statue is thought to be of Mentuhotep I. (*Jo St Mart*)

Intef I

c. 2134–2117 BCE
11th Dynasty

Intef I was the founder of the 11th Dynasty and so, while the Middle Kingdom is generally accepted to have begun when unified under Mentuhotep I (c. 2060–2010 BCE), Intef is commonly grouped with other members of his dynasty. In fact, Intef I was probably barely more powerful than any other provincial *nomarch*, though it appears that his ambitions, and those of his two successors—also named Intef—were vaulting. Having declared himself pharaoh, he adopted the (rather overstated) Horus name of Sehertawy, which means, "He who has brought calm to the Two Lands." In fact, it is likely that this little-known pharaoh brought a number of nomes under his control, including Koptos, Dendera, and three nomes of Hierakonpolis, thus extending his rule and providing a larger power base for his successors.

Right: Funerary stela of Intef I, which shows the goods the pharaoh wished to take with him into the afterlife. (*Jo St Mart*)

Far right: The sarcophagus of Intef I is an excellent example though not so ostentatious as those of later pharaohs. (*Jo St Mart*)

Intef II

c. 2117–2069 BCE
11th Dynasty

Intef II was the younger brother of Intef I, and in keeping with the family's trait, his achievements again appear to have fallen short of his ambitions. While he adopted the Horus name "King of Upper Egypt and Lower Egypt," in all likelihood his triumphs led only to the consolidation of the 11th Dynasty's power in Upper Egypt around Thebes and as far south as the First Cataract, as well as pushing his northern border beyond Abydos to Antaeopolis. His successor, Intef III, brought even more of Lower Egypt under his control, providing the fourth king of the 11th Dynasty with an opportunity to at last realize the hopes of his forebears.

Right: This ornately carved block from the tomb of Intef II shows the pharaoh in the traditional position of offering, holding out a vase in each hand. (*Jo St Mart*)

Mentuhotep I
c. 2060–2010 BCE
11th Dynasty

A militaristic king, Mentuhotep I succeeded in reuniting Egypt. It is thought that the successor of Intef III spent the first years of his reign campaigning in the south in Nubia and turned his attention north after about fourteen years when Abydos rebelled against Theban rule. Mentuhotep I vanquished the revolt and began campaigns that ended with his having brought the whole of Lower Egypt under his heel. That this was a long war is attested to in inscriptions that refer to his being the "Uniter of the Two Lands" by the thirty-ninth year of his fifty-year rule.

Mentuhotep I's conquest is generally held to signal the beginning of the Middle Kingdom and a new prosperity and confidence in Egypt. Construction projects were begun, among them work on his own tomb at Deir el-Bahari. This elegant series of columned terraces stands over a chamber that contained a superb statue of Mentuhotep I when it was discovered by Howard Carter.

Right: Dating to the reign of Mentuhotep I of the 11th Dynasty, this stele is dedicated to Irtysen the sculptor and tells of his ingenious endeavors. (*The Art Archive/Musée du Louvre, Paris/Gianni Dagli Orti/AA390108*)

Mentuhotep II

c. 2010–1998 BCE
11th Dynasty

The son of Mentuhotep I appears to have inherited a peaceful and prosperous country and turned his attentions to making it more so. Surviving inscriptions tell of his trading with Nubia to the south and scouring the land for resources with which to continue the great building works of the pharaohs. Although the final resting place of Mentuhotep II has never been located, it is believed that he was entombed within a chamber carved into the great walls of rock that embrace his father's own temple.

Right: This sandstone funerary statue of Mentuhotep I was discovered in 1899 by Howard Carter. It was encased in fine linen and had the crown of Lower Egypt on its head. (*Jo St Mart*)

Far right: This colorful frieze of Mentuhotep I also shows the pharaoh wearing the high white crown of Upper Egypt. (*Jo St Mart*)

Above: In this marvelously preserved carving, Mentuhotep III is standing in the traditional pose of Osiris, legs close together, arms crossed, and in each hand a crook-shaped scepter and a flail. He is also depicted wearing the holy beard of Osiris. (*Jo St Mart*)

Mentuhotep III

c. 1997–1991 BCE
11th Dynasty

There are few extant records of the final king of the 11 Dynasty, and if his tomb exists at all it has never been found. It is possible that works related to him were expunged or destroyed after he was usurped by his vizier. Indeed, the Royal Canon of Turin which dates to 1200 BCE and lists more than 300 kings, suggests that Egypt was without a pharaoh during the six years that comprised his reign. This is highly unlikely of course, and the fact that Mentuhotep III existed is corroborated by one or two broken relics and an inscription that relates the journey of his vizier, Amenemhet, to quarry a stone for use as the king's sarcophagus.

Amenemhet I

c. 1991–1962 BCE
12th Dynasty

Although it is impossible to state with certainty, the founder of the greatest dynasty of the Middle Kingdom, which would span two centuries, seems to have declared himself pharaoh after dethroning his master, Mentuhotep III. In whatever manner he came to power, however, his reign was an undoubted success. Perhaps conscious of his own betrayal, early in his twenty-nine-year reign Amenemhet I moved to weaken the provincial *nomarchs* and centralize power to himself, then later created a new institution by appointing his son Sensuret I co-regent. Although brought to an abrupt end in his murder, his rule appears to have spread stability and prosperity across Egypt. His tomb at Lisht is a modest pyramid in the style of the Old Kingdom.

Left: The tomb of Amenemhet I is one of the most lavishly decorated of all Egypt's antiquities. Almost every chamber has been painstakingly painted in a number of different styles although time has taken its toll on many. Here is just one of the better-preserved examples. (*Jo St Mart*)

Senusret I

c. 1971–1926 BCE
12th Dynasty

Appointed joint (if junior) pharaoh a decade before his father was murdered, Senusret I reigned for a remarkably long and prosperous time. He was campaigning against Libya to the west when news of his father's murder arrived, and he set forth immediately to quash the coup. Having done so, it appears that his apprenticeship as pharaoh stood him in excellent stead, for in many respects his rule built on the foundations laid by his father. Indeed, monuments, forts, temples, and stele the length of Egypt are testament to the stability of Senusret I's thirty-four remaining years as pharaoh and their inscriptions as well as other relics from this productive period relate that he consolidated the pharaoh's power and extended Egypt's influence in the lands to the south.

Senusret also established mining operations and sponsored a wealth of art, craftsmanship, and literature, including "The Instructions of Amenemhet," a remarkable papyrus within which Amenemhet I passes the principles of kingship to his son. Among the most important of his achievements was the construction of the temple of Re-Atum at Heliopolis. Unfortunately, it has long since gone, though a pair of massive obelisks, dating from later in Senusret's reign, remain.

Like his father before him, Senusret I took a co-regent. Three years before his death, Amenemhet—his son by chief wife Nefru—joined him as joint ruler and Senusret turned his attention to the construction of his own tomb. A pyramid, close by and similar to his father's, it stands over a further nine smaller pyramids built for his wives and daughters.

Above: From what remains of this carved fragment of sandstone, it is possible to make out the pharaoh Senusret I being welcomed or guided by two deities. (*Jo St Mart*)

Amenemhet II

c. 1929–1895 BCE
12th Dynasty

Amenemhet II was interred in a pyramid at Dahshur (now reduced to a shapeless pile of blocks), far from his father and grandfather. In many respects he continued to build upon the traditions of his two predecessors. Treasures and relics from his reign are spread far and wide, suggesting that Amenemhet II exchanged gifts with and created diplomatic ties to Mesopotamia, the Levant, Crete, and Lebanon, and it is also documented that he mounted expeditions to Nubia and the land of Punt. Among the artifacts dating from his reign is a set of records known as the *genut*, or "day books," discovered at a temple at Tod. These recount the daily life of Amenemhet II's court.

Below: The pink granite sphinx with the head of Amenemhet II was discovered in Tanis and dates to the Twelfth Dynasty. (*The Art Archive/Musée du Louvre, Paris/Gianni Dagli Orti/AA381060*)

Senusret II
c. 1897–1878 BCE
12th Dynasty

Senusret II was appointed co-regent by his father, Amenemhet II, in about 1897 BCE, and assumed complete power about three years after his father died. Like those of his immediate forebears, his reign is held to be a peaceful and prosperous one during which stable relationships with the *nomarch* regional governors were cemented by the bestowal of honors and gifts, and trade and diplomacy with Egypt's neighbors increased.

Central to his successful government, perhaps, was Senusret's preference for civic improvement over warfare. Under his rule a program for the expansion of agriculture was pursued, with marshlands being drained and new irrigation systems constructed, particularly around the Faiyum. Senusret II also presided over other improvements in Egypt's infrastructure, including new canals and dams.

In fact, Senusret II appears to have had a great interest in the Faiyum region. It is here that he built his pyramid (now, like his father's despoiled and eroded into a mound of blocks that once would have been the core) as well as a great shrine at Qasr es-Sagha in the northeast of the region. His pyramid is unusual in being the first of its kind to attempt to protect its inhabitant and his accompanying treasures from grave robbers. Its entrance was concealed beneath a pavement at some distance removed rather than being within the wall of the pyramid itself. This did not, however, deter thieves. The tomb was despoiled at some point in the past, though archeologists under the famous British Egyptologist William Matthew Flinders Petrie did later find a fine gold *uraeus* cobra that may have come from the pharaoh's sarcophagus. A later expedition also opened a shaft close by that contained the remains of princess Sit-Hathor-Yunet surrounded by personal effects including jewelry and cases of cosmetics.

Around the time of Senusret II's reign the Middle Kingdom was reaching its cultural zenith, a fact that is attested to by the sophistication and beauty of the artworks produced. Particularly fine examples include a statue of the pharaoh that captures a much more individual expression than was previously the norm, as well as two black granite statues of Nefret, a lady of the court and probably either wife or sister to Senusret.

Right: All that remains of the pyramid of Senusret II in Lahun are mud brick interior walls that are eroding quickly. The casing of limestone was stolen centuries ago. (*Jo St Mart*)

EL LAHOUN PYRAMID
A MUD BRICK PYRAMID.
BUILT BYSENUSERT II.
12 Th DYNASTY.
MIDDLE KINGDOM.
HEIGHT 48M BASE 106M.
ENTRANCE TO THE SOUTH.
اللاهون
بناه الملك سنوسرت الثاني.
مبني من الطوب اللبن.
دولة وسطى.
ارتفاعه ٤٨م
طول قاعدته ١٠٦م
المدخل من الجنوب.

Senusret III

c. 1878–1841 BCE
12th Dynasty

The mightiest of the 12th Dynasty pharaohs, Senusret III was described by the Greek-Egyptian historian Manetho, writing in the 3rd Century BCE, as being over six-and-a-half feet tall, and his reputation looms larger still. In a break with what was now a tradition, Senusret III was never called by his father to sit at his side as co-regent and (though this is pure conjecture) it is possible that the previous pharaoh was concerned about what his son might do with his power. While there are no records of Senusret II waging any war, his son's reign is characterized by martial expansion.

Arrogant and fearsome in politics as well as battle, Senusret III consolidated his power at home by strictly curtailing that of the nomarchs and establishing a new system of bureaucracy that divided Egypt into three administrative regions (waret). These comprised a North, South, and Head of the South (Elephantine and Lower Nubia), each overseen by a council that reported directly to the vizier. And with Egypt firmly under his control, Senusret III was free to turn his attention south.

The distinctly non-martial reigns of his predecessors had seen Nubia gradually extending its influence over Egypt's southern borders (around the Third Cataract). Now, Senusret III launched a series of vicious campaigns over the course of his reign that re-established Egypt's superiority. Indeed, a stele at Semna

Above: Standing in the typical pose of Osiris, this pillar, carved in the likeness of Senusret III, was discovered at the ancient Temple of Amun in Karnak. (*The Art Achive/Luxor Museum, Egypt/Gianni Dagli Orti/AA392606*)

Below: These three black granite statues depict the pharaoh Senusret III. During his reign he was considered a forceful leader, so much so that he was deified by later generations. (*Jo St Mart*)

that dates to the eighth year of Senusret III's rule is inscribed with hieroglyphics that translate as "I carried off their women, I carried off their subjects, went forth to their wells, smote their bulls; I reaped their grain, and set fire thereto." It is unsurprising perhaps that, given the punishment he rained down upon them, Nubians began to worship Senusret III as a god. And where previous pharaohs had built temples

Above: This diorite statue of a sitting Senusret III is thought to have been carved during his youth. It was discovered in the Temple of Medamud. (*Jo St Mart*)

and irrigation channels, Senusret commissioned imposing forts. Even his less obviously martial projects often had a military application. For example, his improvement of the old trade canal around the First Cataract was designed to allow his war fleet easy passage.

Nevertheless, conquest brought plunder, and a portion of this appears to have been spent on refurbishing Egypt's temples and raising new monuments to himself. In fact, though his name is less familiar than other great rulers, Senusret III's image is one of the most widely seen. Carrying on an artistic development that seems to have begun in his father's time, Senusret's features carved into statues do not have the coldly implacable and characterless expressions of times past, but are strikingly individual. Heavily hooded eyes stare piercingly in a face that appears noble yet thoughtful and serious.

As befits a king of his martial arrogance, Senusret III's pyramid at Dahshur is the largest built by the Middle Kingdom pharaohs, though it is possible that he was actually interred elsewhere, at a massive and highly ornate necropolis in Abydos that was held to be the most extensive tomb complex in Egypt until the discovery of the vaults of Ramesses II's sons at the Valley of Kings.

Amenemhet III

c. 1842–1797 BCE
12th Dynasty

The last great king of the 12th Dynasty, Amenemhet III joined his father as co-regent about two years before the latter's death, and probably reigned for a further forty-three years after that. Like those of his father, Amenemhet III's statues are strikingly individual and his features alternate between a strong, proud visage in those carvings associated with the religious aspects of his role and more delicate, sensitive-seeming portraits elsewhere.

His father's martial successes would have gifted Amenemhet III with a strong, stable country, and—like his grandfather—the pharaoh concerned himself with improving Egypt's agriculture as well as with extensive mining. The wealth these policies generated was lavishly spent on construction projects that, it is thought, drained the royal treasury by the time his long rule came to an end.

Notable among the many buildings that he raised are a vast temple dedicated to the crocodile god Sobek at Kiman Faris (a city the Greeks named Crocidopolis), two great statues of himself at Biyahmu, and two pyramids, at Dahshur and

Hawara. The first of these appears to have been abandoned due to subsidence soon after it was completed and Amenemhet III was laid to rest in the pyramid at Hawara, which later became famous as the inspiration for the Labyrinth of Minos. Indeed, the pyramid (now in ruins) contained an astounding network of passages, complete with the trapdoors and concealed passages that might be expected from an Indiana Jones movie.

It is believed that Amenemhet III's reign ended in relative poverty for Egypt, and possibly with the return of famine. Certainly, little is known about his two successors, Amenemhet IV (c. 1798–1786 BCE) and Queen Sobeknefru (c. 1785–1782 BCE). Few records exist for them and there is no convincing proof that the two pyramids sometimes connected to them are actually theirs.

Right: Unlike most pharaohs, Amenemhet III took the decision to build two pyramids, one at Dahshur, which is now badly eroded, and this one, at Hawara, which has fared slightly better. (*Jo St Mart*)

SECTION FIVE
The Second Intermediate Period
(c. 1782–1574 BCE)

As in the First Intermediate Period, records for the second are scarce, not least because Egypt's rulers seem to have been at some pains to obliterate the memory of them. However, it is apparent that a dwindling of power took place during the 13th Dynasty, the glories of the 12th draining away while famine destabilized the nation. Most historians consider the 13th Dynasty to belong within the Second Intermediate Period, though there is evidence among the few monuments and relics that date to this period to suggest that the state of Egypt at this time may not have been quite so parlous as was thought in the past. That said, records for the period are, frankly, a mess. Numerous pharaohs are mentioned on the Turin Canon that are uncorroborated by any other evidence, reigns were short, chronologies conflict, and no two sources are in agreement. It is even likely that few of the 13th Dynasty pharaohs were related.

However, that central government, and the power of the pharaoh, had waned is plain to see in the fact that the short-lived 14th Dynasty, comprising a family governing

Left: Even though Sobekhotep III reigned for only three years a remarkable number of ancient artifacts have been prescribed to him. This stone carving shows the pharaoh accepting offerings. (*Jo St Mart*)

from Xios in the eastern delta, broke away from the official rule. (The obscure 14th Dynasty is thus contemporaneous with the 13th.) Once again, Egypt was breaking apart, and in about 1720 BCE the immigrant Asiatic culture known as the Hyskos seized Avaris, a town close to modern-day Qantir in the Nile Delta. From there the Hyskos slowly proceeded to spread their influence across the north and delta region, eventually founding a foreign dynasty (the 15th).

Little now remains of the Hyskos rule, though it appears that they sacked the old capital of Memphis soon after they had established their rule from Avaris, and grew to such power that the native Egyptian rulers (including the also obscure 16th Dynasty, which encompassed just two pharaohs) were vassal kings. Nevertheless, to the south a new dynasty was rising.

The early pharaohs of the 17th Dynasty in Thebes had few resources with which to attempt a reunification of Egypt. It is perhaps laudable that, sandwiched between two allied and hostile powers—the Hyskos to the north and Nubian Kushites to the south—they managed to preserve their own way of life at all. However, the later pharaohs at Thebes became increasingly intent on reclaiming the delta. Hostilities spilled into war during the reign of Tao II (c. 1574), and his son Kamose (1573–1570 BCE) continued to harry the Hyskos. It was a new king, however, Ahmose I (1570–1546 BCE), who was to finally break the power to the north. The founder of Egypt's 18th Dynasty thus also became the founder of the New Kingdom.

Below: Many rulers also had images of their loved ones carved into their tombs. These two statues are of the 16th Dynasty ruler Qar and his young son. (*Jo St Mart*)

Right: According to Egyptian funerary rites, the "Opening of the Mouth" ceremony would reanimate a mummy or even a statue and allow it to speak and breathe. This painting shows Ay performing such a ritual. (*Jo St Mart*)

Wegaf

c. 1782–1780 BCE
13th Dynasty

The possible founder of the 13th Dynasty is an almost complete mystery to us. Although there do not appear to have been any major disruptions in Egypt about the time of Wegaf's accession—from which it has been deduced that the transition of power from the 12th Dynasty did not cause significant turmoil—almost nothing remains of his reign. In fact, his name is mentioned on just two stalae (one in Nubia and another at Karnak) and a scarab seal. Together with a single statue that may be Wegaf at the Egyptian museum in Cairo, and a mention in the Turin Canon, which relates that he ruled for just over two years, this constitutes the sum of knowledge that modern historians have regarding this pharaoh.

Sobekhotep I

c. 1766 BCE
13th Dynasty

Like so many of Egypt's monarchs of the Second Intermediate Period, there is a certain amount of confusion surrounding Sobekhotep I. The Turin Canon relates that he ruled around 1750 BCE, but historians have scraps of evidence from a handful of ancient papyri that suggest he was actually the first king of the 13th Dynasty, the son of Amenemhet IV and his half-sister Sobkenefru of the 12th Dynasty. Therefore, Wegaf is either fictive or misplaced. Beyond the fact that he was the first king to incorporate the name of the crocodile god into his own, very little is known about him. Sobekhotep I's name is recorded on a dozen monuments.

Right: This brightly painted stela is one of the few remaining items which can be attributed to Sobekhotep I, as much of his more salient records have been lost. *(Jo St Mart)*

Hor I

c. 1760 BCE
13th Dynasty

Thanks to his tomb remaining undisturbed by robbers, the probable twelfth pharaoh of the 13th Dynasty is much less of an enigma than his two predecessors. His pyramid lies close by that of Amenemhet III of the 12th Dynasty at Dahshur and yielded a superb carved wooden statue of the king, now in Cairo's Egypt Museum, along with a wooden sarcophagus bearing his name, and various other funerary objects. The statue is of particular quality and depicts the pharaoh striding forward bearing the arms of ka (the soul) on his headgear. Rock crystal and white quartz were used to create the statue's eyes and lend the image a lifelike quality.

Despite the craftsmanship of the carving, the paucity of the tomb indicates a loss of wealth in Egypt, though may also be due to the brevity of Hor I's reign. The Turin Canon tells us that he ruled for just months.

Right: This wooden ka statue of Hor, the third king of the 13th Dynasty, was discovered in Dahshur. Such icons were meant to provide a resting place for the soul after death. (*The Art Archive/Egyptian Museum of Cairo/Alfredo Dagli Orti/AA325678*)

Right: A view showing more of the whole statue of Hor I. It is believed that he ruled for only a few months and his funeral was somewhat austere compared to those of his fellow pharaohs. (*Jo St Mart*)

Sobekhotep II

c. 1750 BCE
13th Dynasty

Beyond a name in the Turin Canon, a statue that now resides at the British Museum, and a name carved into a block of stone at Abydos, nothing is known of this pharaoh. His reign seems to have been a short one (he is sandwiched between Amenemhet VII and Khendjer in the Turin list of kings), and historians have postulated that he was the son of Sobekhotep I, although with at least seven pharaohs taking the name of the crocodile god during the Second Intermediate Period it is impossible to be sure.

Neferhotep I

c. 1741–1730 BCE
13th Dynasty

Neferhotep I's reign was a relatively long one by the standards of the Second Intermediate Period, and is also comparatively well-documented. Although he does not seem to have undertaken any large building projects, his rule is attested to by two stelae and several statues among various other relics. Listed as the 22nd king of the 13th Dynasty in the Abydos Lists and the 27th by the Turin Canon, it is thought that Neferhotep I was unrelated to previous pharaohs of the 13th Dynasty, but may have been a descendant of Amenemhet III through his mother. His father's position as a powerful temple priest may also have helped him assume kingship. That his reign was moderately successful can be seen in the fact that in increasingly turbulent times he managed to maintain control and consolidate his power over Upper Egypt as far north as the Nile Delta. There is also evidence that he maintained diplomatic channels with foreign powers and mounted mining expeditions into the desert.

Below: Despite his reign being so long ago, many fine examples of artwork and sculpture remain from the times of Neferhotep's rule. This painting is just one fine example of many. (*Jo St Mart*)

Ay
c. 1720 BCE
13th Dynasty

Although sources conflict over the length of Ay's reign, it is widely accepted that he was another pharaoh with no obvious claim to the throne. In fact, it is possible that he was a refugee from the town of Avaris (where his tomb is located), the powerbase of the Hyskos, and it is unclear how he came to rule. It is more certain that during his reign the 13th Dynasty was weakened even further. The Hyskos strengthened their grip on the north and were probably in control as far south as Memphis during Ay's reign. The 13th Dynasty pharaohs that immediately succeeded him appear to have been a motley assortment of nomarchs and regional governors.

Right: Although not thought to be of royal blood, Ay still built himself a pyramid in his home town of Avaris. Now only ruins remain but archaeologists have discovered scarab seals and other items that attest to his long reign. (*Jo St Mart*)

Far right: A view of the interior of Ay's tomb in Avaris. (*Jo St Mart*)

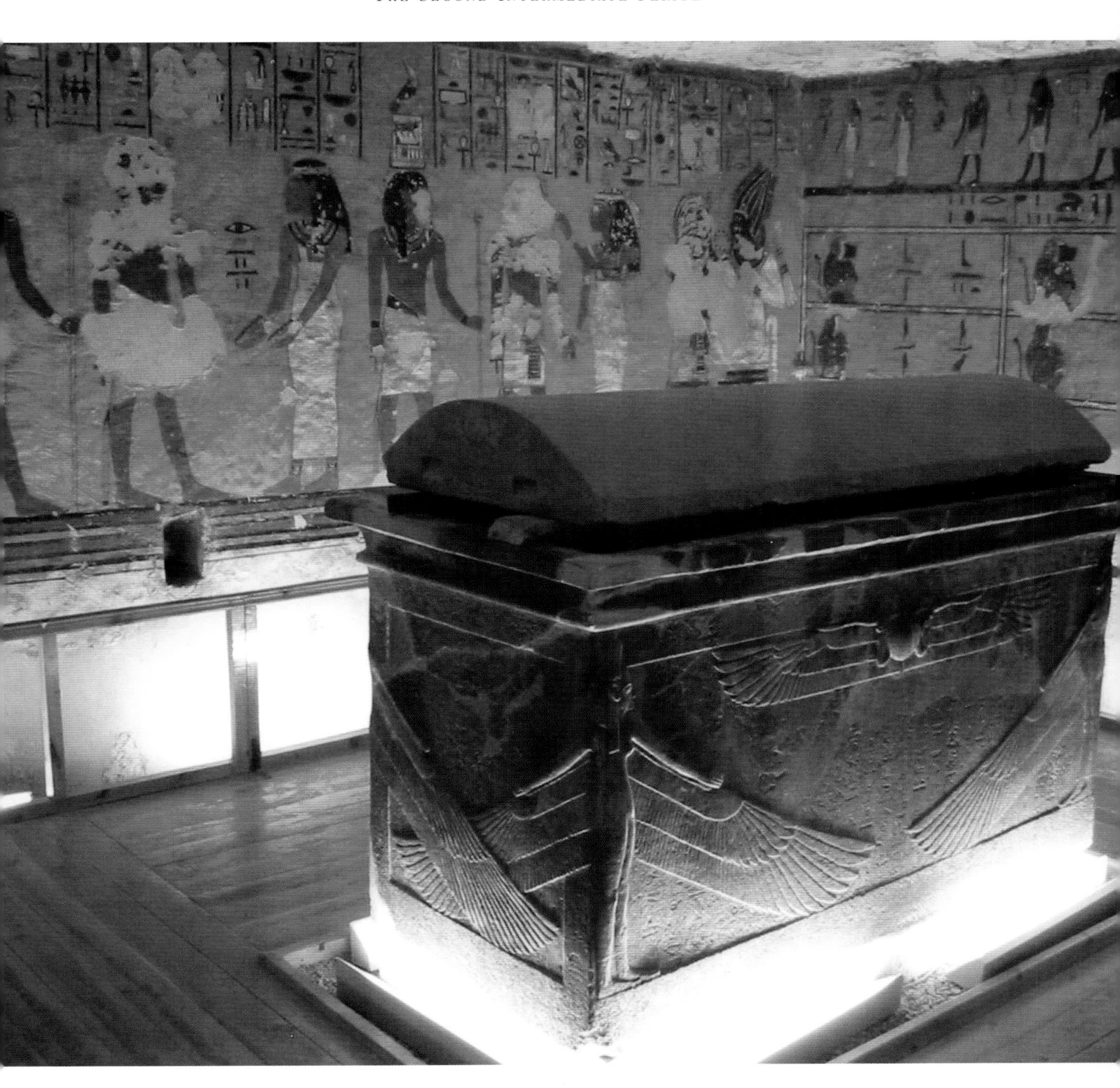

Intef VI

c. 1620 BCE
17th Dynasty

Like the 13th, 14th, and 16th Dynasties, it is presumed that the first kings of the 17th paid tribute to the Hyskos rulers to the north (the 15th Dynasty), and for generations seem to have lived in relative peace alongside their foreign-descended northern masters. Intef VI is thought to be the ninth ruler of the 17th Dynasty, and like his forebears reigned in relative obscurity by permission of the Hyskos. His tomb, however, suggests that more wealth was accumulating at the southern Theban capital, containing as it did a golden sarcophagus along with various other funerary objects.

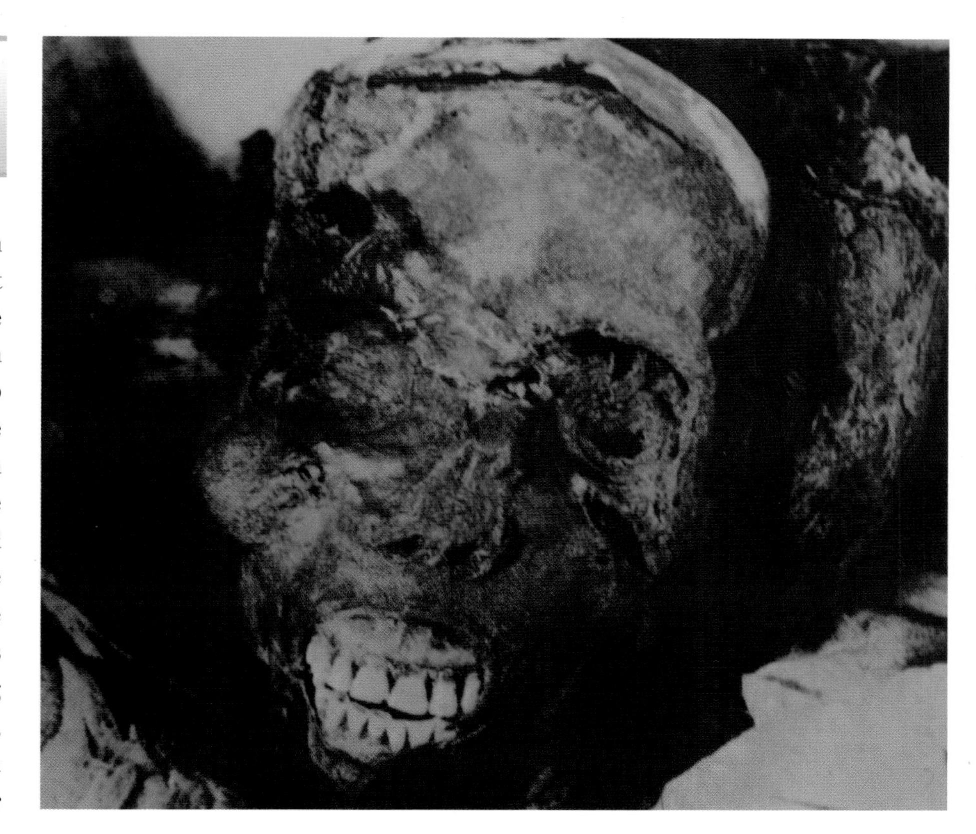

Above right: The mummy of Seqenenre displays evidence of severe wounds. It is thought he was killed by blows from an axe and a spear. His embalming was rushed and possibly done on the battlefield. (*Jo St Mart*)

Left: This gold inlaid sarcophagus is attributed to the pharaoh Intef VII but, since many rulers were named Intef, it is sometimes difficult to distinguish between each one. This example was found in Dra Abu'l Naga. (*The Art Archive/Musée du Louvre, Paris/Gianni Dagli Orti/AA390698*)

Tao II

c. 1574 BCE
17th Dynasty

The severe head wounds apparent on the mummified body of Tao II (whose Horus name Seqenenre means "Who Strikes Like Re") suggest that this king died in battle against the Hyskos. Indeed, he is sometimes referred to as "The Brave." By the time of Tao II's rule the native rulers of Egypt at Thebes had become increasingly hostile to the foreign power controlling the north of their country and Tao is noted for leading his troops in an attempt to reassert Egyptian rule. This war against the Hyskos Dynasty, begun by his father, was continued by Kamose (c. 1573–1570 BCE). However, he, too, would be unsuccessful in ousting the foreign rulers and was entombed at Thebes in a simple burial site with little in the way of funerary objects.

SECTION SIX
The New Kingdom
(1570–1070 BCE)

The third, and greatest, flowering of Egyptian culture witnessed an incredible renaissance. Over 500 years and three dynasties (the 18th to the 20th) the country achieved an unprecedented might and wielded it across the ancient world. Many of the pharaohs of the New Kingdom are the names that are most instantly recognized today—Queen Hatshepsut, Tutankhamun, and Ramesses the Great among them—and many of the temples, fortresses, and monuments that the pharaohs of the New Kingdom raised remain with us still as a reminder of the glory of the Egyptian Empire.

Undoubtedly as a reaction to the rule of the Hyskos, which almost toppled native Egyptian rule for good, the country now began to reinforce its borders and extend them. Particularly under Thutmose III (1504–1450 BCE) and again Under Ramesses II (1279–1212 BCE) the army swelled and new lands came under Egyptian control; notably Nubia far to the south, tracts of the Near East, and Syria. Egypt's pre-eminence on the world stage also brought a massive increase in trade and once more the pharaohs spent much of the proceeds erecting vast monuments to their gods and themselves, including the

Left: A view of the colonnaded courtyard of the Luxor Temple. Built by Amenhotep III, this 300-ft-long corridor contains fourteen columns, each lavishly decorated with tales of the pharaohs. (*Jo St Mart*)

colossal statues of Ramesses II at Abu Simnel. An indication of the wealth of the New Kingdom pharaohs can be found in the fabulous treasures of Tutankhamun's tomb, with its solid gold sarcophagus and famous gold mask. This for a minor boy-king whose unremarkable reign lasted only nine years. How much greater must have been the treasures of great Ramesses II's grave is a question that has tantalized historians since.

Over such a lengthy period there were, of course, occasional reversals of fortune, for example during the reign of Amenhotep IV (or Akhenaten as he renamed himself). A religious fanatic, Akhenaten ruled that the previously minor sun god Aten was to be worshipped exclusively, and devoted himself entirely to Aten's veneration, much to the detriment of Egypt's empire, which shrank as the Hittites took control of Syria and Palestine. However, Egypt recovered from what is now known as the Amarna Period and reconquered, reaching a new peak of power under Ramesses II—power that continued virtually unabated for decades after his death, though corruption and trouble between political factions at court now began to weaken the pharaoh's grip on the country.

Widely held to be the final great pharaoh, Ramesses III (c. 1182–1151 BCE) saw the golden years begin to fade. Beset by military struggles against foreign invaders, the royal treasury again ran dry. His successors were plagued by squabbles over succession, drought, and a mysterious event that saw the sun almost blotted from the sky for over two years (thought now to have been caused by a huge volcanic eruption in Iceland). With corruption rampant and Egypt's empire crumbling, the last pharaohs of the 20th Dynasty lost control of southern Egypt to the High Priests of Amun, while the north now belonged to Smendes, who would go on to found the 21st Dynasty.

Left: The colossus of Queen Hatshepsut at her mortuary temple in Dier el-Bahari. She was the first ruler to choose this site as her burial ground but many more would follow her example, thus earning it the title "Valley of the Kings." (*Jo St Mart*)

Right: This bust represents the young pharaoh Amenhotep II. He is thought to have been an accomplished athlete and to have fathered many children, as many as eleven sons and daughters. His tomb was used as a hiding place for other royal mummies. (*Jo St Mart*)

Ahmose I

c. 1570–1546 BCE
18th Dynasty

The pharaoh destined to overthrow the Hyskos in fact began his campaign against the foreign power only about halfway through his reign, but once started seems to have prosecuted the war with a vengeance, attacking the Hyskos bastions of Avaris and Memphis as well as engaging the enemy elsewhere in Lower Egypt. From the accounts that remain, notably that from the tomb of another Ahmose who served under the pharaoh, the war was bloody and hard fought over many battles. Eventually Ahmose I succeeded in routing the Hyskos from Egypt and even harried the retreating forces as they pulled back to Palestine. Egypt was again united under one pharaoh, and the New Kindgom dawned.

Nevertheless, Egypt was not yet safe, and over the remainder of his reign this hard-pressed king was forced to strengthen his grip over Egypt by holding his borders against

Right: This statue depicts a youthful Ahmose I, the founder of the 18th Dynasty, and dates back to c. 1570 BCE. (*The Art Archive/Musée du Louvre, Paris/Giannni Dagli Orti/AA375077*)

Above: This polished granite statue has been named "Ahmose, Son of Baketre." Very little is known about her, although some jars bearing her name suggest she may have been one of the king's consorts. (*Jo St Mart*)

would-be Syrian invaders and also re-establishing Egypt's old dominance over Nubia. In spite of military necessity though Ahmose I lost no time in returning to the pastime of kings: temple building. Inscriptions at Abydos relate that Ahmose I commissioned several, sadly now lost to us, as are the whereabouts of his own tomb.

Curiously though, we can still look upon the face of the first pharaoh of the New Kingdom. Along with other royal bodies, the mummy of Ahmose I was moved to one of two secret caches by the High Priests of Amun in about 1000 BCE (to protect it from the depredations of tomb robbers) and was uncovered in 1881.

Amenhotep I

c. 1551–1524 BCE
18th Dynasty

In a restoration of the traditions of the 12th Dynasty, Amenhotep I appears to have ruled at his father's side as co-regent during the latter five or six years of Ahmose I's reign. His own rule probably lasted a further twenty-two years, though unfortunately much of the details of it are unknown. However, the same inscriptions in the tomb of the other Ahmose, that relate the story of his father's war against the Hyskos, also provide evidence of further military campaigns under Amenhotep I, notably against Nubia and Libya as well as the Kush, suggesting that though Egypt was now united, the instability of Ahmose I's reign spilled over into that of his son.

Opinion differs as to the location of the pharaoh's tomb, with it being either at Dra Abu el-Naga or a modest complex in the Valley of the Kings depending on which you favor. However, in 1881 his mortal remains were uncovered elsewhere, along with those of his father, at the Mortuary/Memorial Temple of Hatshepsut and now reside at the Egypt Museum in Cairo.

Right: These figures were unearthed around the Temple of Amun. The seated figures represent Amenhotep I while the standing statues are thought to characterize Thutmose II. (*The Art Archive/Gianni Dagli Orti/AA396487*)

Below: The intricately carved and decorated wooden sarcophagus of Amenhotep I now rests in the Egyptian Museum, Cairo. (*The Art Archive/Egyptian Museum, Cairo/Gianni Dagli Orti/AA390964*)

Thutmose I

c. 1524–1518 BCE
18th Dynasty

Although it is possible that Thutmose I was appointed co-regent by Amenhotep I, and likely that he married into the royal line, he is thought to have been a commoner by birth, achieving status through distinguished military service. Indeed, though his reign was relatively short at only six years, it was marked by martial successes—particularly against the Nubians and Syrians—and he extended Egypt's borders "as far as that which the sun encircles," to quote Thutmose I's imposing stele at Abydos.

A prolific builder, Thutmose I raised monuments and temples the length of Egypt, including magnificent new buildings at the Temple of Amun at Karnak. His own tomb in the Valley of the Kings contained two sarcophagi, for himself and his famous daughter Hatshepsut, whom he may also have taken as a wife toward the end of his reign. Curiously though, another tomb complex at Luxor has also been assigned to him and it is possible that Thutmose I's remains were relocated there before being taken to the safety of the cache at Deir el-Bahari, which was discovered in 1881.

Above: One of the two remaining stone obelisks erected by Thutmose I at the Temple of Luxor. Only the base of the second obelisk now remains. (*Jo St Mart*)

Left: This large stela of Thutmose I is now at the Cairo Museum but was discovered in the Temple of Seth at Naqada. (*Jo St Mart*)

Thutmose II
c. 1518–1504 BCE
18th Dynasty

Young and sickly, Thutmose II was the third son of Thutmose I by a minor wife and his unlikely ascension to the throne while still a teenager was due to the untimely death of his older half-brothers. In a bid to shore up his position Thutmose II took his half-sister (and probable step-mother) Hatshepsut as wife, and the two ruled jointly for fourteen years—possibly producing a daughter called Neferure—though some scholars have recently argued that his rule should be shortened to as little as three years. Nevertheless, most Egyptologists agree that the ambitious Hatshepsut was the power behind the throne during his reign, which may have led Thutmose II to name his son (also called Thutmose) by the harem girl Isis as his heir. Various statues and inscriptions of the pharaoh survive, and he usually appears alongside Hatshepsut.

Despite his frailty, a stele at Aswan reports that Thutmose II put down a revolt in Nubia, having many put to death in punishment. The whereabouts of his mortuary complex is a mystery, though his mummy was found at Deir el-Bahari.

Above: The remains of a relief from the tomb of Thutmose II, showing him adopting the traditional position in submission to the gods. (*Jo St Mart*)

Right: The mummy of Thutmose II indicates that he died in his early thirties and had been in poor health. His was one of the many royal mummies found in the cache of 1881. (*The Art Archive/Egyptian Museum, Cairo/Gianni Dagli Orti/AA390969*)

Hatshepsut

c. 1479–1458 BCE
18th Dynasty

Above: Just one of many well preserved examples of statuary depicting a seated Queen Hatshepsut. Several like this were discovered in Dier el-Bahari in immaculate condition. (*Jo St Mart*)

Wife to King Thutmose II and daughter of Thutmose I and Queen Ahmose, Hatshephsut was a powerful and determined woman. Starting her life as royal consort, gaining position as co-regent, then eventually having herself crowned as ruler would not have been an easy proposition.

When her husband died suddenly in the thirteenth year of his rule, Hatshepsut had no sons of her own to assume the throne. Instead the power passed to Thutmose III, the king's infant son by one of the royal harem consorts. His mother, lacking the required royal blood to assume the place of regent, was overlooked and the title was given to Hatshephut. For many years Hatshephut acted as a typical co-regent, allowing her step-son his rightful place in royal affairs and never assuming to over-shadow him. By the seventh year of her regency, however, she had assumed the title of king. Hatshephut was always careful to acknowledge Thutmose III as joint king but made her dominance clear on the many monuments and shrines she went on to build.

Carvings dating back to the time of Hatshephut and Thutmose III show her slow rise to power. In the earlier carvings, Thutmose always stands in front of a humbly dressed Hatshepsut, thus emphasizing her lesser position, but as time passes the carvings change. Soon the two co-regents stand side by side until eventually it is Hatshephut who has the dominant position and Thutmose stands behind her. In order to hold the position of king, she also started to play down her femininity. By doing this she moved away from the perceived image of a consort and also provided an image of strength that her people could believe in. She appears in many statues and drawings with the body of a man. Sometimes she appears with a feminine face but with a decidedly androgynous body.

Early on in her rule the new king quickly stamped out any uprisings from neighboring countries by staging some

quick and decisive military actions in Nubia, Syria, and the Levant, but it seems that the rest of her reign was peaceful. As was fitting for a king of Egypt, Hatshepsut took a queen. Her daughter, Princess Neferure, was called on to assume the role, even taking the traditional titles of "Lady of Upper and Lower Egypt" and "Mistress of the Lands." To further consolidate her claim on the throne Hatshepsut reinvented the tale of her birth, claiming that she was the child of the god, Amun. The deity had fallen in love with her mother and assumed the form of her father so that they might have

Above: This large granite sphinx, now placed in the Metropolitan Museum of Art, bears the likeness of Queen Hatshepsut. She wears the traditional false beard of the pharaoh to symbolize her power. *(Jo St Mart)*

a child. Once born, Amun decreed that Hatshepsut was destined to rule over all Egypt.

During her reign, the country enjoyed a period of great prosperity and peace, as well as a substantial amount of improvements. Hatshepsut reopened the trade routes that

had been suspended during the Hyksos occupation, and trips were made all over the region for building materials, including a now legendary expedition to the bountiful land of Punt (believed to be somewhere around modern-day Ethiopia.) Five ships and over 200 men set out on the long and arduous journey that included a 100-mile march across arid desert while carrying the dismantled boats. The expedition was a great success, however, and the pharaoh's envoys bought back much treasure, including thirty-one frankincense trees. Hatshepsut was so pleased that she ordered a mural be painted on the walls of her tomb at Deir El-Bahari commemorating the epic journey, while several of the trees were replanted in the courtyard.

What Hatshepsut is truly remembered for is her dedication to the rebuilding of Egypt. In fact, she was one of the most prolific builders the country had ever seen. She constructed monuments at Karnak and restored the Precinct of Mut, which had been badly damaged during the Hyksos occupation. She also added two giant obelisks to the temple entrance. At the time they were the largest in the world and to this day scientists have been unable to ascertain just how such enormous stones were hewn, transported, and constructed. Hatshepsut built temples all over Egypt and also in Nubia, Elkab, Armant, and Elephantine island, to mention but a few. By far her most impressive achievement was her mortuary temple at Deir El-Bahari. This majestic colonnaded edifice was built 1,000 years before the Parthenon and was designed by the king's architect and her personal "favorite," Senenmut. (Some recently discovered ancient Egyptian graffiti implies the two were lovers.)

In the twenty-second year of her reign, Hatshepsut died and Thutmose III was able, finally, to assume full

Left: Queen Hatshepsut erected two giant red granite obelisks at the Temple of Amun in Luxor. Now only one remains. (*Jo St Mart*)

control of the throne. Toward the end of his reign, Thutmose seems to have made the decision to erase Hatshepsut from the history records. Her images were carefully removed from many monuments and cartouches. Statues were torn down and smashed into pieces. There was even an attempt to wall in the great obelisks at Karnak. Worst of all, her great mortuary temple was badly defaced. Giant statues of Hatshepsut were pulled down, crushed, and buried in a pit. For many years it was thought that this destruction was an act of revenge by Thutmose II, for being denied the throne for so long, but it seems unlikely he would wait so many years to act. A more plausible theory suggests he was trying to ensure the succession of his son, Amenhotep II, rather than any of Hatshepsut's relatives.

Below: This pillar, situated outside Hatshepsut's enormous mortuary temple, is dedicated to the goddess Hathor. *(Jo St Mart)*

Thutmose III

c. 1504–1450 BCE
18th Dynasty

Despite the difficulties of his early reign, which Thutmose III probably only survived due to his political cunning, the pharaoh outlived his power-hungry step-mother and went on to become one of Egypt's most illustrious rulers. Finally freed from the overweening Hatshepsut in the twenty-first year of his reign, he proceeded to extend his rule over Egypt's neighboring countries, earning him the sobriquet "The Napoleon of Ancient Egypt" from Egyptologists and founding an Egyptian empire that would last for centuries.

It is possible that in one respect at least Thutmose III owed his great conquests to Hatshepsut. Egyptologists agree it is likely that in order to escape her influence he entered military service at a young age, which afforded him an excellent education in warfare as well as friends among Egypt's military leaders.

Once rid of Hatshepsut he wasted no time in making use of his prowess. In the second year of his sole reign he led his troops on a brilliant campaign up the Syrian coast that took Gaza, Yehem, and finally Megiddo. The latter was an exceptional example of strategy. Given a choice between three routes to the city, Thutmose chose a dangerous narrow canyon pass that was ripe for ambush, leading his men from the front to surprise forces that were arrayed to protect the easier routes. The enemy was swiftly beaten and the city was besieged, falling to Thutmose a few months later.

These great victories along the Syrian coast heralded a rule that would be characterized by conquest. In fact, Thutmose III plunged deeper into Syria with every passing year for almost two decades, ferrying troops up the coast on his growing navy and eventually adding 350 towns to his empire.

Like many pharaohs before him, Thutmose III lavished the spoils of his campaigns upon building works, and was particularly fond of steles and obelisks proclaiming his conquests, notably the giant Victory Stele at Karnak. The great 6th and 7th Pylons at Karnak also date to his reign, as do further obelisks there. New temples also arose under his rule, from the distinctive and richly ornamented temple at Karnak known as "Festival Hall" to buildings at Elephantine and Semna in Nubia.

Due largely to the inscriptions

Far left: This red granite statue is believed to be of Thutmose III. As is customary for such sculptures, he wears the high crown of Upper Egypt although much of his facial features have been worn away. *(Jo St Mart)*

Left: A clearer picture of the young pharaoh, Thutmose III, who went on to deface many of his step-mother's monuments after her death. *(Jo St Mart)*

on the many structures he commissioned—and those on the tombs of his courtiers who enjoyed their own share of the great wealth that Thutmose III's reign generated—his is a relatively well documented rule. Chief among his numerous queens was Hatshepsut-Merytre, and others were taken for diplomatic reasons. The pharaoh was also in the habit of making hostages of neighboring princes, later returning them to their homelands well educated in Egyptian ways and obedient to the Egyptian throne. His own son was appointed co-regent for the final three years of Thutmose III's exceptionally long reign, by which time the pharaoh must have been an octogenarian.

Given the scope of Thutmose III's conquests, the length of his rule, and the magnificence of his court, it is surprising that his tomb was a modest one. Located up a cliff face in the Valley of the Kings, its entrance was sealed off with a fall of rocks. Even this failed to protect it though, and by the time it was discovered in 1898 all that tomb robbers had left were a few pieces of broken furniture. Fortunately, the king's wrapped body had been among those removed to the great cache at Deir el-Bahari.

Left: This picture from the reign of Thutmose III seems to show servants picking and filling jars of fruit. (*Jo St Mart*)

Amenhotep II

c. 1453–1419 BCE
18th Dynasty

The son of Thutmose III and Hatshepsut-Merytre, Amenhotep II enjoyed a reign that closely rivaled that of his illustrious father. Inscriptions on a wealth of relics depict him as a great athlete in his youth, whose sporting achievements included shooting arrows through a copper plate while driving a chariot, a deed deemed so magnificent that it is recorded on several steles (including one at Giza and another at Thebes) and it is also found documented as far away as the Levant.

Although a prolific builder (among the temples and monuments erected during his reign were a temple to the god Horemakhet at Giza and a "Festival Hall" at Karnak), aspects of Amenhotep II's reign remain unclear. While he sired many sons, the names of his wives are a mystery, and it is possible that they were kept deliberately obscure to curb the power of women at court following Hapshetsup's usurpation. However, it is evident that the pharaoh ruled over an almost unbroken period of peace and prosperity, notwithstanding rebellions in Egyptian lands in Syria early in his reign. These he quashed swiftly and mercilessly, hanging the bodies of seven princes of the region of Tikhsi upside down from the prow of his flagship and subsequently displaying them on the walls of the Theban temple. A further campaign in Syria appears to have been similarly quick. Such displays of force effectively subdued other potentially aggressive powers. On stele inscriptions various chiefs are shown offering Amenhotep II gifts and allegiance, while there is also evidence of peace treaties with foreign powers.

His resting place in the Valley of the Kings seems to have been used as a minor cache by later priests. Although, like so many others, the tomb had been stripped by robbers, his mummy was found in the company of other royal bodies when it was rediscovered by Victor Loret in 1898.

Above: This black granite bust represents the pharaoh Amenhotep II and dates to c. 1450 BCE. (*Jo St Mart*)

Right: The mummy of Thutmose IV was discovered in his tomb in 1922. He had been buried with his long bow, which can be seen on his stele at Karnak. Unfortunately it was later stolen. (*The Art Archive/Egyptian Museum, Cairo/Gianni Dagli Orti/AA390971*)

Thutmose IV
c. 1419–1386 BCE
18th Dynasty

Thutmose IV is now chiefly remembered for the "Dream Stele" erected between the paws of the Sphinx. The stele relates how, while out hunting, the young prince fell asleep in the Sphinx's shadow and experienced a dream during which the sun god promised Thutmose that he would be crowned pharaoh if he cleared away the sand that had built up around the great monument. Having completed this task the prince duly became king and enjoyed a long and prosperous, if relatively uneventful, reign: at least as far as we know. In fact, not a great deal is recorded of this pharaoh. One or two inscriptions suggest that he may have been forced to deal with minor rebellions in Syria and Nubia, and his construction projects appear to have been geared toward refurbishing and adding to already existing temples and monuments. An example of this can now be found standing in Rome; the 105-ft obelisk begun by his father to be raised at Karnak is the tallest of its kind and was finished by Thutmose IV, who added just a few inscriptions relating to his own reign.

That his kingdom was prosperous is attested to by the fact that numerous sumptuous private tombs date to his reign, suggesting that the economic fruits of a stable empire had filtered downward. His own tomb, though long since plundered, contained a trove of funerary relics, furniture, and a chariot when it was discovered by Howard Carter in 1903. It did not, however, contain the pharaoh. His mummified body had been moved to lie with that of his father.

Right: The dream stele of Thutmose IV tells the tale of the young prince who sat down between the paws of the sphinx and fell asleep. In a dream the sphinx promised to deliver him the throne of Egypt if he cleared the sand from her statue. He did so and the sphinx kept her promise. (*Jo St Mart*)

Amenhotep III

c. 1386–1349 BCE
18th Dynasty

For four decades under the reign of Amenhotep III Egypt reached yet greater heights of wealth and prosperity than even his illustrious predecessors had attained. The son of Thutmose IV and his chief wife, Mutemwiya, Amenhotep III's was another rule that appears to have been troubled by only minor military spats, allowing the country to develop economically, step up mining operations, and trade far and wide. The benefits of this can be seen in the wealth of art and architecture that survives from this period, as well as in references to the opulence with which the pharaoh surrounded himself.

Although Amenhotep III appears to have taken many wives (mostly the princesses of neighboring or vassal states for diplomatic reasons, though it is thought that he also married two of his own daughters), his first and chief bride was Tiy, the daughter of a provincial governor, to whom Amenhotep III appears to have been greatly attached. Certainly they had at least six children together and she is named many times alongside her husband on memorials and scarabs that relate the king's achievements. Notable among them is a reference to a great lake that Amenhotep ordered dug for his wife's amusement at the Malkata palace at Thebes. She is said to have enjoyed sailing on it.

With the aid of his chief architect, also called Amenhotep, the pharaoh was a prolific builder. Sadly, many of his works have since been destroyed or demolished, but many fine images of him remain alongside a few great monuments such as the two Colossi of Memnon at Luxor, one of which is reported to have made a keening sound at daybreak and sunset each day for hundreds of years. Although there are various accounts of this phenomenon it has not been heard since Roman times. Though time has not been kind to these figures it is still possible to see the pharaoh sitting placidly with hands on his knees and flanked by the smaller figures of his mother and Queen Tiy. In fact, many representations of Amehotep III still exist in a better state of repair than the Colossi, and the pharaoh is represented with composed features that seem to reflect the peace that descended on Egypt during his reign. Equally imposing must have been the Malkata palace, which is now completely lost save for a few broken remains of frescoes that once adorned its walls, and the temple to Amun that Amenhotep III ordered to be built at

Luxor. Although this has also been largely demolished, a superb colonnaded court has fortunately survived. Designed by Amenhotep the architect, it is a magnificent work, massive, yet graceful.

The mummy most commonly held to be that of Amenhotep III was discovered with those of his father and grandfather. His own tomb in the Valley of the Kings was despoiled long ago. Close by was the mummy of Queen Tiy.

Far left: A bust of Amenhotep III wearing the white crown of Upper Egypt and carved from pink granite. This large piece of antiquity was discovered in his temple at Thebes. (*The Art Archive/Luxor Museum, Egypt/Gianni Dagli Orti/AA360760*)

Below: This limestone relief shows Amenhotep III riding a chariot with the vulture goddess, Nekhbet, protecting him from above. (*The Art Archive/Egyptian Museum, Cairo/Alfredo Dagli Orti/AA325680*)

Akhenaten (Amenhotep IV)

c. 1350–1334 BCE
18th Dynasty

Akhenaten is a unique and fascinating figure among the list of Ancient Egypt's kings and queens. An iconoclast and (apparently) a religious fanatic, he adopted a very different rule to that of his forebears and he would be repudiated as a heretic by those who came after him.

The second son of Amenhotep III and Queen Tiy (he was predeceased by an older brother), Amenhotep IV displayed a religious fervor that may have had its roots in politics. It is thought that toward the end of his reign Amenhotep III was becoming concerned that the power of the High Priests of Amun was growing to eclipse his own, a concern that his son must have shared. Indeed, there is compelling evidence that he was elevated to co-regent during the final years of his father's reign.

When Amenhotep III died his son assumed sole rule, and for a short while adopted the rituals and traditions of the previous pharaohs, being crowned at the Temple of Amun at Karnak. Not long after, though, the new pharaoh overturned Egypt's entire religious system by insisting that there was but one god—Aten, a previously insignificant aspect of the sun god Re-Harakhte—with whom the pharaoh alone had the power of intercession. Changing his name to Akhenaten (meaning "servant of the Aten") to reflect this belief, the pharaoh ordered a new temple built at the gates of the temple of Amun, which was closed soon after, and founded a new city—named Akhenaten also, between Memphis and Thebes at modern-day el-Amarna—from which to rule. The significance of his actions cannot be overstated, for Egypt's pantheon had evolved over more than 2,000 years and the pharaoh's role encompassed upholding maat, which implies continuity. Suddenly, however, at Akhenaten's whim, Egypt was a monotheistic realm.

Having imposed his beliefs on the nation, the pharaoh appears to have devoted the remainder of his life to the service of his god, allowing his empire to crumble around him. In practice this left two men in power: Akhenaten's vizier and father-in-law Ay (is believed to have been the father of Queen Nefertiti), and the military commander Horemheb. Both would later use their positions as a springboard to the throne.

The schism with the past can be clearly seen in

artworks of the time, which become suddenly imbued with an unprecedented realism. Gone were the idealized and composed features of previous sculpture. Instead, Akhenaten and his court were carved in a new style. The athletic figure of previous pharaohs was replaced by rounded bellies and sagging chests, while the face of Akhenaten and his courtiers appear much more human, if strangely elongated, a physical trait that some Egyptologists ascribe to extensive incest within the royal family.

The whereabouts of Akhenaten's body can only be guessed at. Although it was the king's wish to be interred within a tomb in his own sacred city, there was no trace of his remains when it was opened in the 1880s or those of his family for whom surrounding tombs had also been cut. It seems likely that Akhenaten's death precipitated an almost immediate outcry against his religious reforms and his body may have been moved to protect it.

Far left: This statue representing Akhenaten has sparked much debate. Due to his unusual features, questions have arisen regarding his ancestry. (*Jo St Mart*)

Right: Another depiction of Akhenaten with the familiar elongated physiognomy. At first there was much speculation that his appearance denoted a genetic disease, but his wife and daughters are also depicted in a similar fashion, suggesting that it was merely a new artistic style. (*Jo St Mart*)

Tutenkhamun

c. 1333–1324 BCE
18th Dynasty

Apart from the eponymous "curse," little is known about either the reign or death of Tutenkhamun, and much of the information concerning him is based on conjecture and guesswork. It is thought that he was the son of Akhenaten and grandson of Amenhotep III, though the identity of his mother is also somewhat of a mystery. Akhenaten's chief wife was Queen Nefertiti and as far as historians can discern she gave birth only to daughters. It is assumed that one of the other queens of court was Tutenkhamu's mother, and the most likely candidate is the so-called Kiya. She seems to have been one of the pharaoh's particular favorites during the first nine years of his reign, but then disappears from records after the eleventh year. Many historians consider it possible that she died in childbirth.

Tutenkhamun ruled as pharaoh during the 18th Dynasty between 1333 BCE and 1324 BCE. When installed as king he was just nine years old and alone. There seem to have been no close family members to protect and support him. As a result he was solely under the influence of his closest advisors—Ay, the political man, and Horemheb, the military advisor.

The king's original name was Tutenkhaten, meaning "Living image of Aten," the name of the god adopted with such fervor by Akhenaten, his father. Shortly after becoming king his name was changed to Tutenkhamun, a clear message to his

name was Ankhesenpaten and she was older than her husband, having already had a child to her father, Akhenaten, making her also a half-sister to Tutenkhamun.

Very little documentation regarding Tutenkhamun's reign has survived to this day, but some of his major achievements have endured, such as re-establishing Thebes as the capital city and undertaking large scale building works at Karnak and Luxor, such as the Great Colonnade and the relief scenes of the Festival of Opet. He also re-opened all of the Amun temples, lifted the ban his father had placed on the old deities, and restored the priesthood. Despite the discovery of a painted box depicting Tutenkhamun's glorious and no doubt victorious

Above: The gold-covered throne of the young pharaoh. The detailed back panel shows his wife, Ankhesenpaaten, helping Tutenkhamun to dress. (*Jo St Mart*)

Left: The opulent funerary mask of Tutenkhamun, which covered the pharaoh's mummified head. (*Jo St Mart*)

Right: This beautifully gilded wooden shrine was discovered in the treasury room of Tutenkhamun's tomb complex. (*Jo St Mart*)

people that he was rejecting the new religion established by his father and returning to the old ways. No doubt this move was orchestrated by his advisors, who witnessed the chaos that the previous king's new religion wreaked across the country.

Surprisingly, Tutenkhamun was married. His wife's

forays against the Nubians and Syrians, it is unlikely that the young boy-king would have ever ventured into battle.

Sadly, Tutenkhamun died very young. In fact, recent forensic tests carried out on his mummy indicate that the pharaoh was just seventeen years old at the time of his death. More testing has been carried out in order to discern the exact cause of his death, and though it was originally thought he died of tuberculosis new analysis shows a tiny bone fragment lodged inside his skull, indicative of a blow to the back of his head. Obviously, the forensic scientists cannot tell if this blow was a result of an accident or a deliberate attack. Such ambiguity only adds to the mystery surrounding the boy-king.

Now a young widow following the unexpected death of her husband, Ankhesenamen found herself in a very tricky situation. With no children from Tutenkhamun, it was left to her to continue the royal line. (Royal succession was traditionally carried through the female line in Egypt.)

Below: A statue from Tutenkhamun's tomb showing the pharaoh dressed as the god, Amun. (*Jo St Mart*)

Right: A closer view of Tutenkhamun's golden throne. Such lavish decoration and treasures were abundant inside the pharaoh's resting place. (*Jo St Mart*)

Surrounded by ruthless men, all much older than she and not the most attractive marital prospects, she made a bold move. She wrote a letter to the king of the Hittites, Suppiluma, asking him to send one of his many sons to become her husband. At first the king was highly suspicious of such an astounding offer, so sent out his spies to verify the queen's story. Once her situation was confirmed he sent a Hittite prince called Zannanza to Egypt. Unfortunately he never made it. Zannanza was assassinated before he reached the border. It seems likely that either Horemheb or Ay ordered him killed in order to keep a grip on the Egyptian throne.

The discovery of Tutenkhamun's tomb in 1922 by English archaeologist Howard Carter shed much light on the life of the little-known king, and the wondrous riches found within caught the attention of the world. The burial chamber contained an enormous granite sarcophagus and inside this were a further three coffins nesting inside one another. The final central coffin was made of solid gold and weighed an incredible 242 pounds. Inside were the remains of the young pharaoh. On his head lay the now famous solid gold funerary mask that weighs 22.6 pounds. Unfortunately, due to an unsatisfactory embalming, the mummy was in a miserable condition. In fact, the condition of the tomb and its treasure seemed to point to a hurried and unexpected funeral. Many of the items in Tutenkhamun's tomb seem to have been intended for someone else. For example, the sarcophagus box had been re-cut to remove the original carvings, and new ones added.

Much of the treasure is obviously from funerary stock, and the size of the tomb itself is too small for a king. It is clear that no one expected to bury such a young pharaoh. Perhaps the most personal and moving items found in the tomb were the mummified remains of two female foetuses, one approximately five months and another around eight months. Historians believe they are the daughters of the young pharaoh. Had either of these children survived they would have taken their place as queen thus continuing the Armana blood line and changing the entire course of the 19th Dynasty.

Horemheb

c. 1321–1293 BCE
18th Dynasty

Little is known of Horemheb's personal history save that he was raised at Herakleopolis and ascended through the military ranks during the rule of Amunhotep III, becoming the commander-in-chief of Egypt's army during the reign of Akhenaten. He was a man of obvious talents and ambition, and it is possible that he was appointed co-regent during the rule of Tutenkhamun as it seems very likely that, with the vizier Ay, he was the power behind the throne during the boy-king's early years. This probability has led to conjecture that Ay and Horemheb may have been involved in Tutenkhamun's death. The pharaoh's reaching maturity would have curbed the power that they had become used to wielding since the days when Akhenaten withdrew from politics to commune with his god. Speculation aside, it is certainly a matter of record that Ay took the throne after Tutenkhamun (possibly while Horemheb had his hands full with campaigning against Hittite forces in Syria). Following Ay's death Horemheb declared himself king, swiftly moving to consolidate his position by marrying a divine adoratrice of Amun, who may also have been the sister of Akhenaten's chief wife Nefertiti.

Once on the throne, Horemheb's reign was less military in character than might have been expected of this old warhorse. He adopted a "divide and conquer" tactic by splitting Egypt's army in two, appointing a commander each for Upper and Lower Egypt (also presumably ensuring that neither would rise to the same degree of power that he had enjoyed). However, other than one or two minor campaigns against the Hittites that may have been concluded in a peace treaty, there is no evidence of Horemheb making a concerted attempt to reassert Egyptian dominance over the region.

Instead, the pharaoh appears to have concentrated on finishing the reversal of Akhenaten's religious reforms. Although Egypt had been moving back to its traditional ways under the two previous pharaohs, it is widely believed that it was Horemheb who completed the restoration and reopening of the temples of Amun (appointing military men as priests in order to be sure of their loyalty), the tearing down the temple of Aten, and the beginning of the demolition of the city of Akhenaten. It is worth noting

Left: Like many rulers before him, Horemheb has himself depicted as a sphinx. *(Jo St Mart)*

Right: The decorations in Horemheb's tomb display more sophisticated art work than in earlier funerary temples. *(Jo St Mart)*

that stones thought to come from Akhenaten have been found used as the foundations to Horemheb's own construction projects, such as the Hypostyle Hall at Karnak.

In addition, he was much concerned with stamping out corruption throughout Egypt. A famous stela on the Tenth Pylon at Karnak carries the "Great Edict of Horemheb," which suggests there were severe penalties for any servants of the pharaoh involved in any corrupt dealings, including the nose being cut off followed by exile.

If we include the years during which Horemheb helped steer Egypt through the difficulties of Akhenaten's reign and ruled in Tutankhamun's stead, he must have exerted a great deal of influence over the country for up to an astonishing six decades. Obviously, the full story of his deeds will never be available to us, yet it is possible that just such a ruthless, strong man was exactly what the country needed to stave of complete disintegration during difficult times. Nevertheless, despite his long life, he appears to have produced no heir and instead named northern vizier Paramess (who would adopt the name Ramesses I) as his successor. For this reason, kings of the 19th Dynasty regard Horemheb as the founder of their dynasty. Although he had previously commissioned an ornate tomb for himself at Saqqara, it is likely that this was before he became pharaoh, since he was eventually laid to rest in the Valley of the Kings.

Ramesses I

c. 1293–1291 BCE
19th Dynasty

As his was a short and relatively uneventful reign, Ramesses I is now chiefly remembered as the father and grandfather of greater pharaohs, and as the founder of the 19th Dynasty. Although, as mentioned previously, evidence suggests that later kings held Horemheb to have begun their line (probably in gratitude for raising the former vizier to the throne), scholars agree that the line should begin with the first Ramesses.

In fact, Horemheb appears to have chosen a staunch ally to succeed him and one that he could be sure would continue his work to restore Egypt's traditions. Ramesses' lowly birth (he is thought to have been the son of an army officer from Avaris) would have counted for less in the eyes of another army commander who ascended the throne than his ability to preserve the country's integrity. Rising gradually through military, religious, and civil ranks under his sponsor, Ramesses may eventually have been appointed co-regent at the end of Horemheb's rule.

Although his short reign (he was thought to be in late middle age by the time he was crowned) means that Ramesses I would have had little time to stamp his mark on Egyptian history, he did commission the construction of a small temple at Abydos and was interred, with little ostentation, in the Valley of the Kings. As an interesting footnote to his reign, a mummified body thought likely to be that of Ramesses I was found thousands of years later being exhibited to crowds at the Niagara Falls Museum and Daredevil Hall of Fame. Once scientists had established that there was a distinct possibility it was in fact the mummy of a pharaoh, the body was returned to Egypt.

Below left: A relief from Ramesses I's chapel in Abydos. Seti I built and dedicated the shrine to his late father. *(Jo St Mart)*

Below: The tomb of Ramesses I was discovered in 1817 and is surprisingly small for the tomb of a pharaoh. *(Jo St Mart)*

Seti I

c. 1291–1278 BCE
19th Dynasty

Seti I was one of Egypt's great builder-kings and a pharaoh of vision and martial might. His reign heralded another great renaissance in Egyptian culture, which would be cemented by his son Ramesses II.

In all likelihood Seti I began his reign as co-regent alongside his father and quickly showed his military mettle. A campaign in Palestine during his father's lifetime was followed by numerous others across Egypt's sphere of influence, including Syria, the Lebanon, and Nubia. Inscriptions on the walls of the temple of Amun at Karnak (as well as stele elsewhere) relate how Seti conquered town after town up the coast toward Syria and later turned his attention to a rebellion in Nubia where he took hundreds prisoner. His mission, it seems, was to restore Egypt to the glories she had known under Amenhotep III and forever expunge the blot of Akhenaten. In fact, in an extraordinary list of Egypt's kings that Seti I commissioned at Abydos, the period now known as Amarna (comprising the reigns of Akhenaten, Tutankhamun, and Ay) are

Above: The temple of Seti I in Abydos has many highly decorated niches, each dedicated to a different Egyptian god. (*Jo St Mart*)

Right: Seti's is the largest of the Abydos temples. Built from limestone it has seven interior sanctuaries instead of the more usual one or two. (*Jo St Mart*)

stripped from Egyptian history completely, the succession jumping directly from Amenhotep III to Horemheb.

Like many pharaohs before him, Seti I appears to have equated Egyptian greatness with the magnificence of her buildings and the largesse of her gods, among whom he counted himself. During his rule construction began on many works that rival others any in Egypt and often surpass former splendor. Perhaps the most famous example is the Hypostyle Hall of great carved columns in the Temple of Amun at Karnak, and the carved reliefs in the walls there that recount his military victories, but the Temple of Seti I at Abydos is rightly held to be one of the marvels of Ancient Egypt. Here the pharaoh commissioned a temple that held seven sanctuaries. One was dedicated to himself and the others to Osiris, Isis, Horus, Re-Harakhte, Amun-Re, and Ptah. Complete with remarkable carved reliefs and paintings that show the pharaoh in his role as representative of the gods, the temple demonstrates a full return to Egypt's ancient ways and also would have served to establish the son of an army commander as the rightful king. Behind the temple a unique building known as the Osireion was built. Comprising a long underground tunnel leading to a vast hall, it was here that Seti I's body laid in state before being taken on its final journey to the Valley of the Kings.

Here too, the pharaoh outshone his predecessors. His tomb is among the greatest in the valley. Discovered in 1817, it is an extraordinary complex of booby traps, false walls, and hidden entrances plunging 300 feet into the rock. It is a tragedy that all these safeguards did not deter tomb robbers, yet the lavish paintings and carvings that ornament Seti I's tomb are beyond compare. More fortunately, his body was among those found at Deir el-Bahari in 1881 and is an excellent example of the art of mummification.

Below: Many of the decorations on the wall of Seti's temple depict the pharaoh making offerings to the gods. *(Jo St Mart)*

Ramesses II

c. 1279–1212 BCE
19th Dynasty

Ramesses II dominates Ancient Egyptian history like one of his colossal statues at Abu Simbel. Also known as Ramesses the Great, he is, undisputedly, the most illustrious of all the pharaohs. During a reign that spanned seven decades he proved himself an able warrior and was the consummate Egyptian builder-king. Aided by good fortune (or the indulgence of the gods), Egypt flourished under his rule as never before. The Nile flooded regularly, harvests were excellent, and the arts and architecture reached new heights of brilliance. Over it all loomed the refined and composed face still so familiar over 3,000 years later.

In fact, statues of the pharaoh must have been something of an exercise in public relations. His mummified body reveals that the actual face of the great king—long and blessed with a large, beaky nose—bears little resemblance to the many statues of him. Curiously, tests of the pharaoh's dyed red hair show that he was a natural red head in his youth, a very rare coloring among the Ancient Egyptians.

In early life Ramesses would have been highly trained in the art of warfare. Given his father's martial disposition and his future role as Egypt's protector it would have been unthinkable for him not to have joined Seti I on various campaigns, and while co-regent he was given his own command. His first known military campaign was to

Below: When first discovered in 1813, the giant statues of Ramesses II were so encased in sand that archaeologists didn't know whether they were standing or sitting. (*Jo St Mart*)

cleanse Egypt's northern shores of pirates. Having done so successfully, he turned his attention to reinforcing Egypt from invasion, building a chain of fortresses along the northwestern border.

The pharaoh's ambition though was not protection, but expansion, specifically in Syria, southern parts of which had been won by Thutmose III, lost during Akhenaten's rule, conquered again by his father, and were now crumbling away once more. It is, however, somewhat difficult to ascertain the success of his campaigns. There were early victories, such as the conquest of the kingdom of Amurru, but Ramesses II's wars of expansion were ultimately halted at the Battle of Kadesh. Although Ramesses claimed this as a great victory it is thought that the pharaoh came close to being killed or captured and the massive Egyptian and Hittite forces fought each other to a truce. Despite this, Egypt under Ramesses the Great was as large, if not larger, than at any point in its history, and her military might and a network of truces and alliances helped maintain a generally peaceful environment that nurtured prosperity at home.

Below: This is one of two giant granite heads found in the temple of Ramesses II at Thebes. It is 8.9 feet high. (*Jo St Mart*)

In common with his forebears, Ramesses II used the proceeds of a prosperous nation, as well as booty from his campaigns, to finance building projects. His, however, were on an unprecedented scale. In fact, the whole of Egypt is littered with temples and monuments erected by Ramesses (and others originally belonging to former pharaohs to which he would casually add his own name). Among the greatest are his massive extensions to the temples of Luxor and Karnak and the Ramesseum at Thebes, which contains the massive black granite head of Ramesses that moved the poet Shelley to pen the immortal lines, "My name is Ozymandias, King of Kings: Look on my works, ye mighty, and despair!" Tens of thousands of laborers, including the Hebrews, were set to work on building sites and quarries along the length of the country. As an interesting aside, although there is no Egyptian record of the matter, it was on Ramesses II that Moses is thought to have brought down God's plagues and from whom he led his people away to the Promised Land.

Ramesses' most famous construction is, of course, the Great Temple at Abu Simbel. Cut directly into the rock face at its entrance sit four vast statues of the pharaoh, designed

Above: A small fragment of a relief depicting Ramesses II. (*Jo St Mart*)

Below: One of the smaller but richly painted chambers from the interior of Ramesses II's mortuary temple. (*Jo St Mart*)

to dwarf anyone entering and underline the might and divinity of the king. Within are further statues of the pharaoh as Osiris, and deep inside are four seated gods. So incredibly accurate was the construction that twice a year, at the equinox on February 22 and October 22, the morning sun pierces the temple to illuminate three of them. The last is of Ptah, god of the underworld.

Building was not the only arena in which Ramesses II displayed his extravagance. With eight principal wives among his harem, the pharaoh claimed to have fathered about a hundred sons and even more daughters, three of whom he later married, along with his sister. His first, favorite, and best-known wife, however, was Nerfertari whose tomb in the Valley of the Queens at Thebes contains some of the most exquisite paintings of the era.

It is thought that Ramesses II was 91 or 92 at his death and he was laid to rest in the tomb he had commissioned in the Valley of the Kings. As might be expected, it is the largest complex to be found there. Sadly, it has deteriorated over time, although the ornamentation is not so rich as the almost equally large tomb of Seti I. It was, of course, robbed of the treasures it once contained thousands of years ago, but the extravagance of the funerary objects for Egypt's greatest king must have been incredible to behold. Like many other royal mummies, Ramesses II's escaped the looting, however, and was found at Deir el-Bahari in 1881.

Below: The carefully mummified remains of Ramesses II, the great pharaoh and builder of some of Egypt's most imposing architecture. (*Jo St Mart*)

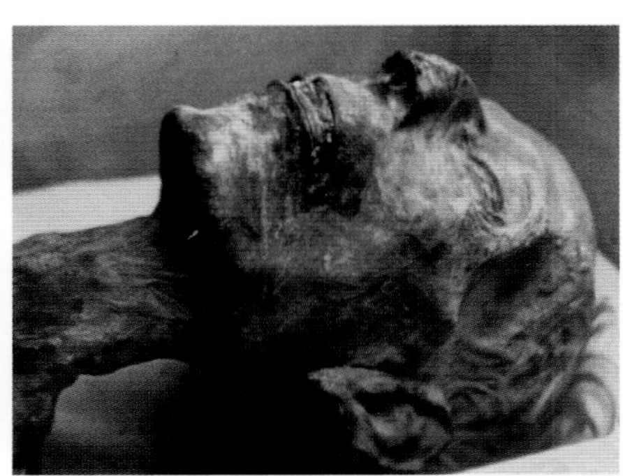

Merneptah

c. 1212–1202 BCE
19th Dynasty

The reign of Ramesses the Great's thirteenth son Merneptah is generally accepted to have been a relatively short and uneventful one, particularly in comparison to that of his father. Having outlived twelve of his older brothers, Merneptah would have been elderly himself by the time he was crowned. Fortunately, in light of later events, his early career was in the military and his experience there served him well as pharaoh. The little we know of his reign comes primarily from inscriptions at the Temple of Amun at Thebes. These relate that Merneptah was beset by revolts and invasions, most probably due to vassal states taking advantage of political upheaval on the death of Ramesses II. It appears that he dealt with these swiftly and ruthlessly.

Left: This giant red granite statue depicts Merneptah wearing the tall crown of Upper Egypt. (*Jo St Mart*)

Amenmesses

c. 1202–1199
19th Dynasty

There is much confusion surrounding the reign of Amenmesses. What little evidence we have suggests that he may have been a son of Merneptah (by a minor queen) and this son usurped the throne while his father was fighting abroad. Some scholars believe that he was simply a Kushite governor called Messuwy, who set himself up as king. Whatever the circumstances, Amenmesses' reign appears to have been a short one of only two or three years, while the fact that many of the small number of relics that bear any mention of him—including those in his tomb at the Valley of the Kings—appear to have been defaced or erased, indicates that he was vilified at the time.

Right: All that remains of a limestone statue of Amenmesses is this head, which is now safely in the Metropolitan Museum of Art. *(Jo St Mart)*

Seti II

c. 1199–1193
19th Dynasty

With peace restored to Egypt during his father's reign, it appears that Seti II inherited a stable kingdom from Merneptah to which he added little in the way of building works. In fact, Seti II seems to have been something of a "caretaker" king, though his tomb is notable for having been open since ancient times and, judging from the graffiti found there, a tourist attraction for the Romans. Interestingly, carvings of his name within the tomb were expunged and then replaced at a later date, while references to Amenmesses in his own tomb have been replaced by the name of Seti II.

Right: A replica statue of Seti II. *(Jo St Mart)*

Below: The temple of Seti II is considerably smaller than other funerary temples. It is speculated that he died before its completion. *(Jo St Mart)*

Siptah

c. 1193–1187
19th Dynasty

Another short-lived pharaoh, Siptah is thought to have been the young son of Seti II and a minor queen called Tiaa. Siptah ascended the throne due to the premature death of an older half-brother. It appears that, given his age and his own early death, Siptah was never able to stamp his mark on the kingdom. Indeed, little is known about him now save the fact that he seems to have been afflicted with a club foot, and it is probable that, although Siptah was pharaoh in name, Egypt was actually governed by his step-mother Twosret and her chancellor, Bay, during his nominal reign. Nevertheless, Siptah was interred in the Valley of Kings, and evidence in and around the pillaged tomb suggests that he was laid to rest alongside his mother.

Above: The sparse interior of the tomb of Siptah where visitors can now view his sarcophagus. (*Egyptian Tourist Board*)

Twosret

c. 1187–1185 BCE
19th Dynasty

The final pharaoh of the 19th Dynasty was recorded by Manetho as having reigned for seven years, but this figure almost certainly includes the six years in which Twosret governed in her step-son's name. Thus her own sole rule would have been a single year. As is so often the case, Twosret is something of an enigma to us today. There is evidence that she had her former chancellor Bay executed toward the end of Siptah's reign and it is thought that her own reign foundered in the civil war that would establish Setnakhte as the founder of the 20th Dynasty. Beyond that, she is little mentioned, and her only known building work, a temple next to the Ramesseum at Thebes, was unfinished. Her own tomb on the Valley of the Kings appears to have been later appropriated by Setnakhte.

Below: A painting from the tomb of Queen Twosret. Her tomb was later reused by Setnakhte, the first pharaoh of the 20th Dynasty. (*Jo St Mart*)

Setnakhte

c. 1185–1182
20th Dynasty

Above: Although he only ruled for four years, Setnakhte has an impressive and lavishly decorated tomb. (*Jo St Mart*)

Ths warrior king is, again, something of a mystery, though he appears to have risen from a catastrophic end to the 19th Dynasty to found the 20th. It is believed that Twosret's reign ended in civil disorder, with Egyptian cities under siege from foreigners, and that Setnakhte was the military leader who repelled the invaders and restored order, taking the crown as his reward.

Ramesses III

c. 1182–1151 BCE
20th Dynasty

The first years of the Ramesses III reign were uneventful, yet everything changed in his fourth year as pharaoh. Trouble began when the Libyans, allied with the Meshwesh and the Sped tribes, tried to invade the Western Delta, no doubt tempted by the lush terrain that was so much more bountiful than the desert they inhabited. The Egyptian army won a resounding victory, killing most of the invaders and putting any survivors into slavery, and it would be another four years before any threat would endanger Ramesses III.

The next great battle over Egypt came from an unlikely source. During the eighth year of Ramesses III's kingship, the people of the surrounding countries began marching towards Egypt. Having suffered many droughts, and desperate to settle in the land of plenty, a huge force of different tribes known as the "Sea Peoples" made their way to the Delta. This was not an army but families—women and children, oxen and carts piled high with belongings—

Below: One of the large statues of Ramesses III found in Karnak. *(Jo St Mart)*

all seeking somewhere better to live; it could be described as a well armed exodus. Once again, Ramesses III and his army destroyed the "invaders," taking an enormous amount of wealth back to the priests of Amun, swelling their coffers. This wealth would later have catastrophic consequences in the next dynasty and split Egypt in two.

Right: Lying on the Theban foothills is the Medinet Habu, which holds the mortuary temple of Ramesses III. (*Jo St Mart*)

Below: One of the many ornate reliefs found in the Medinet Habu. (*Jo St Mart*)

Ramesses IV

c. 1151–1145 BCE
20th Dynasty

Ramesses IV was given the title of "crown prince" by his father, Ramesses III, following the early deaths of his four elder brothers. Because his father enjoyed such a lengthy reign, almost thirty years, it is believed that Ramesses IV must have been in his forties by the time of his succession, but the new pharaoh nonetheless began a series of ambitious construction projects, including enlarging the Temple of Khonsu at Karnak and, naturally, commissioning a massive mortuary temple for himself. Unfortunately, his reign was cut short when he too, like his brothers, suffered an early death. His tomb, situated in the Valley of the Kings remained unfinished, and his mummy was discovered in the royal cache at Amenhotep II's tomb in 1898.

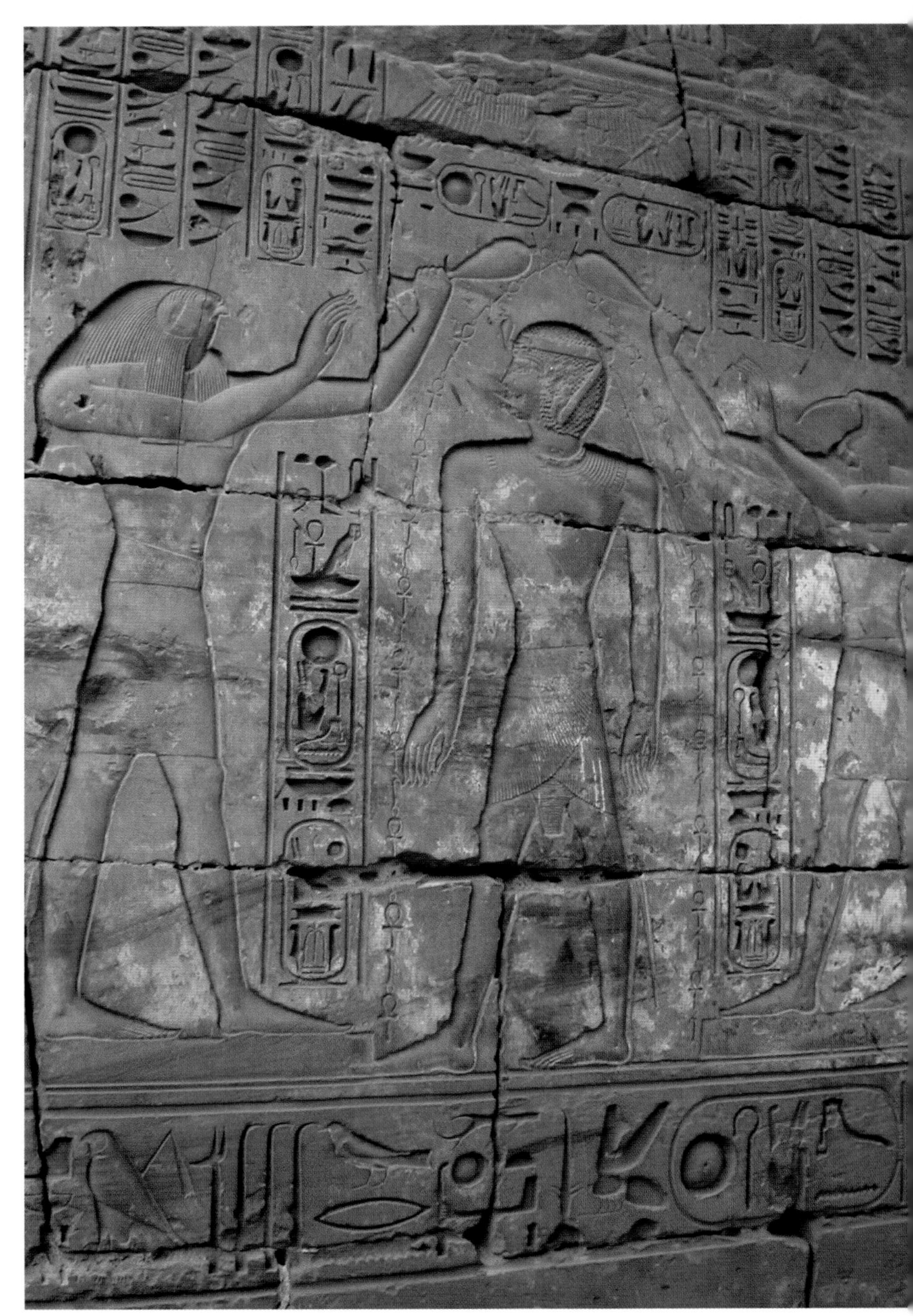

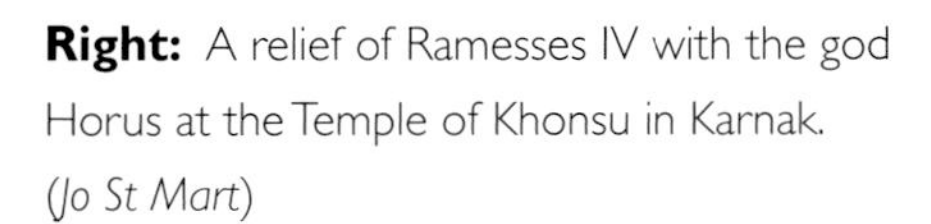

Right: A relief of Ramesses IV with the god Horus at the Temple of Khonsu in Karnak. *(Jo St Mart)*

Ramesses V

c. 1145–1141 BCE
20th Dynasty

The son of Ramesses IV and Queen Tentopet, Ramesses V also suffered a short sovereignty and an early death like his father, though he ruled for nearly four years before Ramesses VI became pharaoh. This was a troubled time for Egypt, with many towns suffering at the hands of Libyan raiding parties. Records tell of the atrocities committed by these bandits, including the burning of the entire town of Per-Nebyt and all its people. Experts surmise that his brother seized the throne in the same way that he also stole his brother's tomb in the Valley of the Kings. Little evidence remains as to how Ramesses V died or how his brother came to take the throne before his death, but Ramesses V died two years into his brother's reign and his mummy was later found in the tomb of Amenhotep II. Investigations show he had lesions on his face, leading to the theory that he died after contracting smallpox.

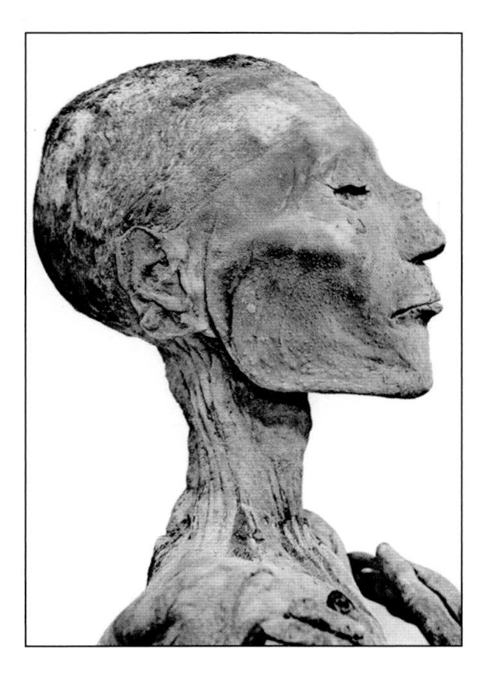

Above right: The mummy of Ramesses V, which was discovered inside the tomb of Amenhotep II. (*Egyptian Tourist Board*)

Left: An ancient statue depicting the face of Ramesses VI. Little remains of the pharaoh's mummified remains as grave robbers hacked it to pieces with an axe. (*Jo St Mart*)

Ramesses VI

c. 1141–1133 BCE
20th Dynasty

The fifth ruler of the 20th Dynasty, Ramesses VI enjoyed a relatively long rule compared to those of his brothers, but for eight years he presided over an increasingly unstable Egypt. The fortunes of his country were floundering and its borders shrinking. The turquoise mines at Sinai were forsaken and the eastern border, which once reached Palestine, now stopped at the bank of the Delta. When Ramesses VI died in 1133 BCE he was interred in his tomb and succeeded by his son, Ramesses VII, but he was not allowed to rest in peace for very long. Grave robbers entered the tomb and desecrated his remains. His hands and feet were chopped off in order to steal the decorative jewelry, and his head and body had been hit several times with a vandal's axe.

Ramesses IX

c. 1126–1108 BCE
20th Dynasty

Ramesses IX was the eighth monarch of the 20th Dynasty and governed for eighteen years. Little evidence regarding his sovereignty remains apart from a few documents and some building works concentrated in the Heliopolis sun temple in Lower Egypt. In fact, many of his projects centered on that region, giving rise to speculation that the High Priests of Amun in Thebes had already garnered a great deal of power in Upper Egypt. This authority would later lead to outright mutiny under the 21st Dynasty. Ramesses IX's reign is also remembered for the many tomb robberies that took place. In his sixteenth year as pharaoh many royal and noble tombs in the western Theban necropolis were violated and raided, including that of King Sobekemsaf I. The offenders were captured and brought to justice. The confessions of Amenpnufer and his six accomplices were recorded on papyrus and it is certain that they all received a death sentence.

Left: This relief of Ramesses IX is now held in the Metropolitan Museum of Art. *(Jo St Mart)*

Ramesses XI

c. 1098–1070 BCE
20th Dynasty

Ramesses XI was the final king of the 20th Dynasty and remained on the throne for twenty-nine years. However, during this time another power grew in the south: Upper Egypt was now under the unequivocal rule of the priests of Amun. A civil war raged between the two factions, with the king governing from his capital in the north, Piramesse, and the High Priest Amenhotep ruling from Thebes. Now that the pharaoh was no longer in control of the vast Nubian gold mines, many tombs were stripped of their riches in order to augment the waning economy. By the nineteenth year of Ramesses XI's reign, Herihor, a military man and later a priest of Amun, had usurped the position of High Priest and installed himself in many high ranking offices, including viceroy of Kush and vizier. This made him an almost invincible authority in the south. However, Herihor never managed to take the throne. Instead, the two parties settled for an unspoken understanding. Herihor's influence would not reach into Lower Egypt and the pharaoh would not wage an ill-advised and expensive war against Thebes.

Left: This earring was found in the tomb of a woman belonging to the court of Ramesses XI. *(The Art Archive/Egyptian Museum Cairo/Alfredo Dagli Orti/AA325717)*

The High Priests of Amun

Although the High Priests of Amun had not claimed the title of pharaoh, it is clear that during the 21st and 22nd Dynasties they effectively ruled Upper Egypt and were equal in power to the king. When Herihor became the High Priest in 1080 BCE, the priests possessed the richest areas of Egypt. They owned sixty percent of the temple lands, almost all of the country's ships, and a large majority of the factories. While the rest of the country was suffering a severe economic downturn, Thebes prospered. Herihor was succeeded by his son-in-law, Piankh, who ruled Thebes for four years before his son, Pinedjem I, succeeded him. Pinedjem ruled in tandem with King Smendes I. He never sought to overthrow the pharaoh, and as a result the accepted co-regency remained peaceful.

Left: Sarcophagus of a priestess of Amun-Ra, c. 1000 BCE. in the Smithsonian's National Museum of Natural History in Washington, D.C. (*via Wikipedia*)

Right: At the Museum of Cairo stands this sarcophagus of Harsiese, who for some time was thought by some to have been a High Priest of Amun, whereas later research suggests that he was an ordinary priest called Harsiese A (albeit an independent king at Thebes during the first decade of Osorkon II's kingship), and that another person given the name Harsiese B was the genuine High Priest of Amun. (*via Wikipedia*)

Harsiese

c. 870 BCE

Although never an official pharaoh of Egypt, Harsiese declared himself ruler of Upper Egypt shortly after becoming the High Priest of Amun at Karnak, around the fourth year of Osorkon II's reign. His actions meant that Egypt was again divided. However, he did not retain his self-appointed title for very long as evidence suggests that by the twelfth year of Osorkon II's rule the pharaoh had regained control of Thebes, the capital city of the south. The implication is that Harsiese had died by that time.

Section Seven

The Third Intermediate Period

(1070–525 BCE)

With the death of the Ramesses XI, Egypt again split in two. At Thebes, Herihor (1080–1074 BCE), High Priest of Amun, had already assumed power over Upper Egypt, beginning a ruling line of high priests that would last almost many decades, while in the Delta Smendes declared himself king at Tanis (his position was cemented through marriage to one of Ramesses XI's daughters), and thus ushered in the 21st Dynasty. In the years that followed the bankrupt country would be riven by civil war and strife, and would suffer increasing numbers of foreign incursions.

Reunited once more under the Libyan-descended Sheshonq I (c. 945–924 BCE), who began a line of pharaohs known as the "Libyan" or "Bubastite" Dynasty (the 22nd Dynasty) after the city of Bubastis in the Eastern Delta from whence they came, Egypt prospered briefly again and Sheshonq brought Israel and Judah under his heel. By the reign of Sheshonq I's grandson, Takelot I (c. 889–874 BCE), however, the country was splintering once more into two separate powers: at Thebes in 870 BCE the High Priest of Amun, the pharaoh's cousin Harsiese, set himself up as a rival king to Osorkon II (c. 874–850 BCE).

Left: The solid silver sarcophagus of Psussennes I was found inside a giant black granite coffin in 1939 by Pierre Montet. *(Jo St Mart)*

Questions of succession would plague the dynasty thereafter. In 818 BCE another prince of royal blood proclaimed a new dynasty (the 23rd) at Leontopolis in the Central Delta, which meant two dynasties reigning separately within Egypt. This situation became more confusing with further fracturing and the rise of the short-lived 24th Dynasty at Sais. Meanwhile, Nubian influence had been steadily pushing northward and in about 732 BCE the Nubian ruler Piankhi (c. 747–716 BCE) took advantage of Egyptian internal bickering and invaded the Delta. He was met by a coalition of no fewer than four Egyptian kings, whom he defeated, bringing Egypt under foreign rule once more (the 25th, or "Nubian," Dynasty), though the extent to which Piankhi and his successors embraced Egyptian culture is witnessed in their elaborate tombs.

However, elsewhere in the world a new power was rising: Assyria. By the time Piankhi's son Taharqa (c. 690–664 BCE) ascended the throne Egypt was under almost constant attack from the new invaders. Conquest was not quick. In fact, Egypt held out against Assyria until about 664 BCE, when Taharqa's cousin Tanutamun ruled from (c. 664 to 656 BCE), but from that time onward Egypt was under the Assyrian yoke, with the 26th Dynasty being client kings and vassals to the Assyrian monarch. Nevertheless, the country was eventually brought together again under one king, Psamtik I, who ruled from Sais, and became increasingly stable and prosperous once more under him and his successors.

By now though the might of Assyria had been eclipsed by legendary Persia. No nation, it seemed, could stand against the Persians, and Egypt was no exception. In 525 BCE Psamtik III met the Persian army at Pelusium, and was crushed. He was later executed at the Persian capital of Susa by order of the Persian king Cambyses II (525–522 BCE), who now added "pharaoh of Egypt" to his list of titles. The 27th Dynasty is also known as the First Persian Period.

Smendes I

c. 1069–1043 BCE
21st Dynasty

In spite of his founding the 21st Dynasty, the origins of King Smendes I are clouded in mystery, though it is believed that during the reign of Ramesses XI he was an influential governor based in Tanis. He legitimized his claim to the throne by marrying one of the daughters of Ramesses XI, and during a twenty-six-year reign he moved the capital of Lower Egypt from Piramesse to Tanis and embarked on an extensive rebuilding of the city. Due to the unhealthy economy, he recycled monuments taken from other cities to ornament his capital. He also rebuilt the outer walls around the temple of Luxor, thus saving it from flooding.

Right: This statue is believed to be a representation of the first pharaoh of the 21st Dynasty, Smendes. (*The Art Archive/Egyptian Museum, Cairo/Alfredo Dagli Orti/AA326325*)

Psusennes I

c. 1039–991 BCE
21st Dynasty

Psusennes I was the son of the High Priest Pinedjem I and one of Ramesses XI's daughters, Henuttawy. Perhaps it was because of his origins that Psusennes I sought to reunite the rival Egyptian states of the north and south: he was the first pharaoh to allow his daughter to marry a High Priest of Thebes and it seems that relations between the royal court and the Amun temples improved during his rule. Proof of this thawing in affairs can be seen in his capital city, Tanis, where Psusennes I built a temple dedicated to the gods Amun, Khonsu, and Mut. In return, the high priests were generous in their donations for the pharaoh's own tomb. When his intact tomb was discovered in 1940 it was full of fabulous treasures, many of them pillaged from other tombs found in the Valley of the Kings, an area under the control of the Amun priests. Such riches would not have been taken without permission from the high priest himself.

Right: The gold funerary mask of Psusennes I, though impressive, lacks the grandeur of Tutenkhamun's. (*Jo St Mart*)

Amenemope

c. 993–984 BCE
21st Dynasty

The son of Psusennes I and Queen Mutnodjemet, Amenemope first ruled as co-regent with his father, then succeeded to the throne after his father's death in 991 BCE. All evidence points to a reign of nine years. It was perhaps a testament to the declining fortunes of Egypt that the tomb of Amenemope was far less luxurious than his father's. In 1940 Pierre Montet discovered the untouched grave in Tanis, where it was one of the few left unspoiled by either robbers or ensuing dynasties seeking to recycle the treasures inside. Montet noted that, whereas Amenemope's father's tomb was large and bedecked with gold leaf, and his mummy was protected by a solid silver sarcophagus, the tomb of Amenemope was smaller and contained a wooden coffin, while his funerary mask was made of gilt rather than gold.

Right: Compared to those of previous rulers, Amenemope's golden face mask lacks fine detail. (*Jo St Mart*)

Siamun
c. 978–959 BCE
21st Dynasty

As well undertaking widespread building works across Egypt, including enlarging the Temple of Amun in Tanis, renovating the Temple of Horus at Mesen, and commissioning construction in Piramesse and Heliopolis, Siamun is probably best known for initiating a more proactive attitude to foreign diplomacy, and was one of the first pharaohs who saw the advantage of marrying Egyptian princesses to close foreign powers. Before Siamun it was more common for foreign princesses to be brought into Egypt, but the pharaoh reversed the trend and cemented an alliance with King Solomon of Israel by sending his daughter to the biblical king. An apparently wise king then, Siamun is also thought to have been responsible for relocating many mummies from their original tombs in the Valley of the Kings, and placing them in hidden, more secure, grave sites beyond the reach of marauding looters.

Left: Part of a relief that tells of Siamun's many conquests and other important achievements of his reign. (*Jo St Mart*)

Below: In this tiny silver figurine, Siamun is depicted as a sphinx. (*The Art Archive/Musée du Louvre, Paris/Gianni Dagli Orti/AA390155*)

Psusennes II

c. 959–945 BCE
21st Dynasty

Precious little is known about the reign of the 21st Dynasty's final king, Psusennes II. Even the length of his reign has been disputed by various Egyptologists: some scholars, taking Manetho as their guide, assign him fourteen years while others credit him with as many as thirty-five. Some believe he was also known as Psusennes III, a High Priest of Amun, which would have made him the first pharaoh to rule both Upper and Lower Egypt since the death of Ramesses XI. His daughter, Maatkare, was married to Sheshonq I, successor to Psusennes II and the founder of the 22nd Dynasty.

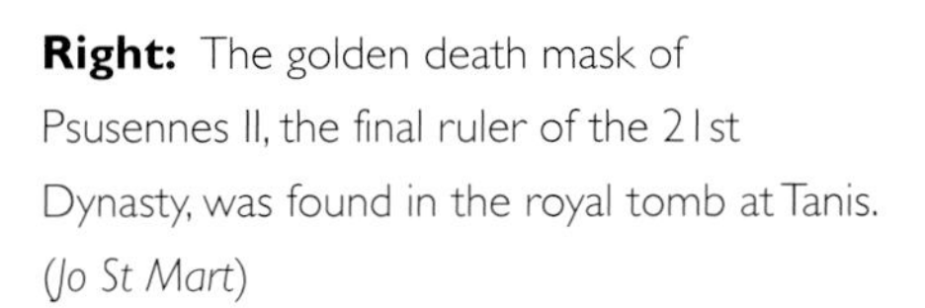

Right: The golden death mask of Psusennes II, the final ruler of the 21st Dynasty, was found in the royal tomb at Tanis. *(Jo St Mart)*

Sheshonq I

c. 945–924 BCE
22nd Dynasty

Sheshonq I was the first king of the 22nd Dynasty—often referred to as the Libyan Dynasty—and the son of a great chief of the Meshwesh, the ancient Libyan tribe that hailed from Cyrenaica. Before becoming the first of many kings who came from there, Sheshonq I had become the leader of all Egypt's armies and his time in the military made him a strong and determined leader. By placing his sons in important positions, and surrounding himself with people he could trust, this foreign-descended pharaoh reunited Upper and Lower Egypt and began the process of reclaiming the country's lost empire.

Above: The funerary mask of Sheshonq, discovered in the royal tomb at Tanis. (*The Art Archive/Egyptian Museum Cairo/Gianni Dagli Orti/AA391013*)

Osorkon I

c. 924–889 BCE
22nd Dynasty

Egypt continued to strengthen under the careful leadership of Osorkon I who—following his father's lead—kept Upper and Lower Egypt united by the simple expedient of placing his son, Sheshonq II, in the position of High Priest of Amun at Karnak. Osorkon I then seems to have concentrated on building many temples, particularly in his home city of Bubastis. In around 890 BCE Sheshonq II joined his father as co-regent but unfortunately died before he could take the throne. The king would eventually be succeeded by Takelot I, another son born to a lesser wife.

Above: This granite statue, unearthed in Byblos, bears the cartouche of Osorkon I. (*Jo St Mart*)

Osorkon II

c. 874 –850 BCE
22nd Dynasty

Osorkon II came to the throne around the same time that his cousin, Harsiese, inherited the High Priesthood at Thebes. Soon after, Harsiese declared himself King of Upper Egypt and once again the country was split in two. Fortunately for the pharaoh Osorkon II, his rival died in 860 BCE, and to ensure his hold on the throne and the reunion of both Egyptian states, Osorkon II replaced him with his own son, Nimlot. But, as well as internal threats to his power from Thebes, Osorkon II also had to deal with the ever increasing menace of Assyria. After conquering Mesopotamia and Syria, Egypt was next, and Osorkon II was forced to do battle with the Assyrian king, Shalmeneser III. Nevertheless, by forging an alliance with their neighbors, Israel and Byblos, Egypt defeated the Assyrian army at the Battle of Qarqar.

Right: This red granite relief features Osorkon II and his wife, Queen Karomama I. *(Jo St Mart)*

Taharqa

c. 690–664 BCE
25th Dynasty

The 25th Dynasty is also known as the Nubian or Kushite Dynasty. The Nubians had embraced the religion of Amun, and slowly their influence in Thebes began to grow until eventually they were able to usurp the throne. Taharqa was the fourth Nubian pharaoh and it was he who had to face an increasingly powerful Assyria. Although he was a brilliant military tactician and repelled the invading armies several times, defeat was inevitable. King Assurbanipal of Assyria pillaged Memphis and put to death many nobles, while Taharqa took sanctuary at Thebes until even that great city became unsafe. He eventually fled Egypt and returned to Nubia, where he died in 664 BCE.

Left: This large granite statue shows the pharaoh Taharqa nestled between the legs of a ram, one of the animals used to represent the god Amun. (*Jo St Mart/British Museum*)

Section Eight

The Late Period and Ptolemaic Egypt

(Late Period 525–332 BCE) (Ptolemaic Egypt 305–30 BCE)

Persian rule of Egypt for a time marked a period of relative prosperity for the country, particularly under the satrap (from Old Persian, "protector of the province") of Darius I (521–486 BCE), during which it was opened to the wider world as never before. Nevertheless, its citizens chafed under foreign rule, and soon after the Greeks dealt Darius a stunning blow at the Battle of Marathon in 490 BCE, Egypt took full advantage and rebelled in 486 BCE. Persia's harsh reaction quashed the revolt, but another broke out in 480 BCE and was again brutally put down.

The next seventy-five years were marked by troubled peace followed by guerrilla warfare, until Amyrtaeus (404–399 BCE), the only pharaoh of the 28th Dynasty, had weakened Persian influence sufficiently to declare himself king. Beyond this, little is known of the man who brought Egypt back under native rule, but the five pharaohs who followed him (within the 29th and 30th Dynasties) would be the last truly Egyptian monarchs. Some historians suggest that the history of Ancient Egypt ends with the

Left: A depiction of Ptolemy IX helping the gods Isis, who is kneeling on the ship, and Horus, who stands behind the sail. (*Jo St Mart*)

Above: Although badly damaged this bust is generally believed to be a representation of Ptolemy X Alexander. (*Musée du Louvre, Paris*)

passing of its last native ruler, Nectanebo II (360–343 BCE). His reign certainly marked a return to traditional Egyptian values and the old ways.

The Persians returned in force in 343 BCE, however, ending Nectanebo's rule and ushering in the very brief Second Persian Period. Brief because in Macedonia a young man destined to become the greatest conqueror the world had ever seen was growing to maturity.

After the death of his father Philip II of Macedonia in 336 BCE, the twenty-year-old Alexander invaded Persia and comprehensively trounced Darius III at Issus in 333 BCE. Continuing his tour of conquest, the young king was in Egypt by 332 BCE and was welcomed as the deliverer from the Persians, a living god and pharaoh. Having founded Alexandria, the conqueror moved on and died less than a decade later. After a further decade (by 311 BCE) his heirs were dead, and Ptolemy, son of Alexander's boyhood friend Lagus, took control of Egypt. By 305 BCE, following war and political intrigue across the ancient world, Ptolemy had married a daughter of Nectanebo II and thus cemented a claim to the Egyptian crown.

The kings and queens who followed Ptolemy I would be the last god-kings of Egypt. Although she was briefly outlived by her son and nominal co-regent Caesarion (36–30 BCE), the days of the pharaohs, which had begun over 3,000 years in the past, finished at the hands of Cleopatra VII (51–30 BCE). She took her own life rather than become a prize for the Roman invaders.

Right: Ptolemy XIII in the guise of Horus at the temple of Kom Obo. Kom Obo is dedicated to Sobek and Horus. It was started Ptolemy VI and finished off by Ptolemy XIII. (*Egyptian Tourist Board*)

Psammethicus I

664 BCE – 610 BCE
26th Dynasty

Due to the long-distance rule of Assyria, Psammethicus I began his fifty-year reign as the king of Athribis and his father, Nekau was named king of Sais by the Assyrian conquerors. When Nekau died in 664 BCE the Assyrian leaders declared Psammethicus king of all Egypt and bestowed on him the tasks of controlling the warring princes of the Delta and making peace with Thebes. He accomplished both tasks. First, he had his daughter and Divine Adortrice of Amun, Princess Nitocris, work closely within the administration of Mentuemhet, an important noble of Thebes, thus ensuring stability through religious ties. He then turned his attention to the princes. He put together a huge army of conscripted men and mercenaries, mainly from Greece, to control any rebellious parties. Under his rule, Egypt saw a return to old religious values and artwork and once again became a major player in the Near East.

Right: Psammethicus I making an offering to the god Ra-Horakhty, a combination of the gods Horus and Ra and considered to be the god of the rising sun. (*Jo St Mart*)

Psammethicus II

595 BCE–589 BCE
26th Dynasty

Very little evidence remains pertaining to the short rule of Psammethicus II. He inherited the throne from his father Nekau II but reigned for only six years. He is known to have marched into Nubia in 592 BCE, making it as far south as Third Cataract. This foray is thought to be in retribution for the deliberate defilement of Egyptian monuments, including that of his father. It is alleged he also sent an army into southern Palestine in 592 BCE to aid Zedekiah, the Babylonian king of Jerusalem. Little else worthy of note remains of Psammethicus' rule and the throne passed to his son, Wahibre, in 589 BCE.

Right: Originally erected in Heliopolis, the obelisk of Psammethichus II now stands in central Rome. (*Jo St Mart*)

Left: An imposing image of Psammethichus II standing beneath a protective Hathor, the cow goddess. To either side sit Isis and Osiris. (*The Art Archive/Egyptian Museum, Cairo/Gianni Dagli Orti/AA391024*)

Above: This fragment from the Metropolitan Museum bears the name Psammethichus II. (*Jo St Mart*)

Ahmose II

570 BCE–526 BCE
26th Dynasty

Following the disastrous military expeditions of Wahibre, the son of Psammethicus II, the army turned against its king and civil war broke out in Egypt. The army looked to one of its own to lead them against the king, a brave general by the name of Amasis, also known as Ahmose II. When the rebels met the royal army in 570 BCE, the king was killed and Ahmose took his place. Under his rule Egypt became relatively peaceful, and Ahmose II instigated many laws to help the country become a more tolerant and

multi-ethnic place. He declared Naukratis a free zone and granted foreigners the right to trade within the city—even temples to foreign gods were permitted. This peaceful period was, however, just a small respite. Soon after there would be another threat to the country: Persia. The mighty empire sweeping across the continent had cast its gaze toward Egypt.

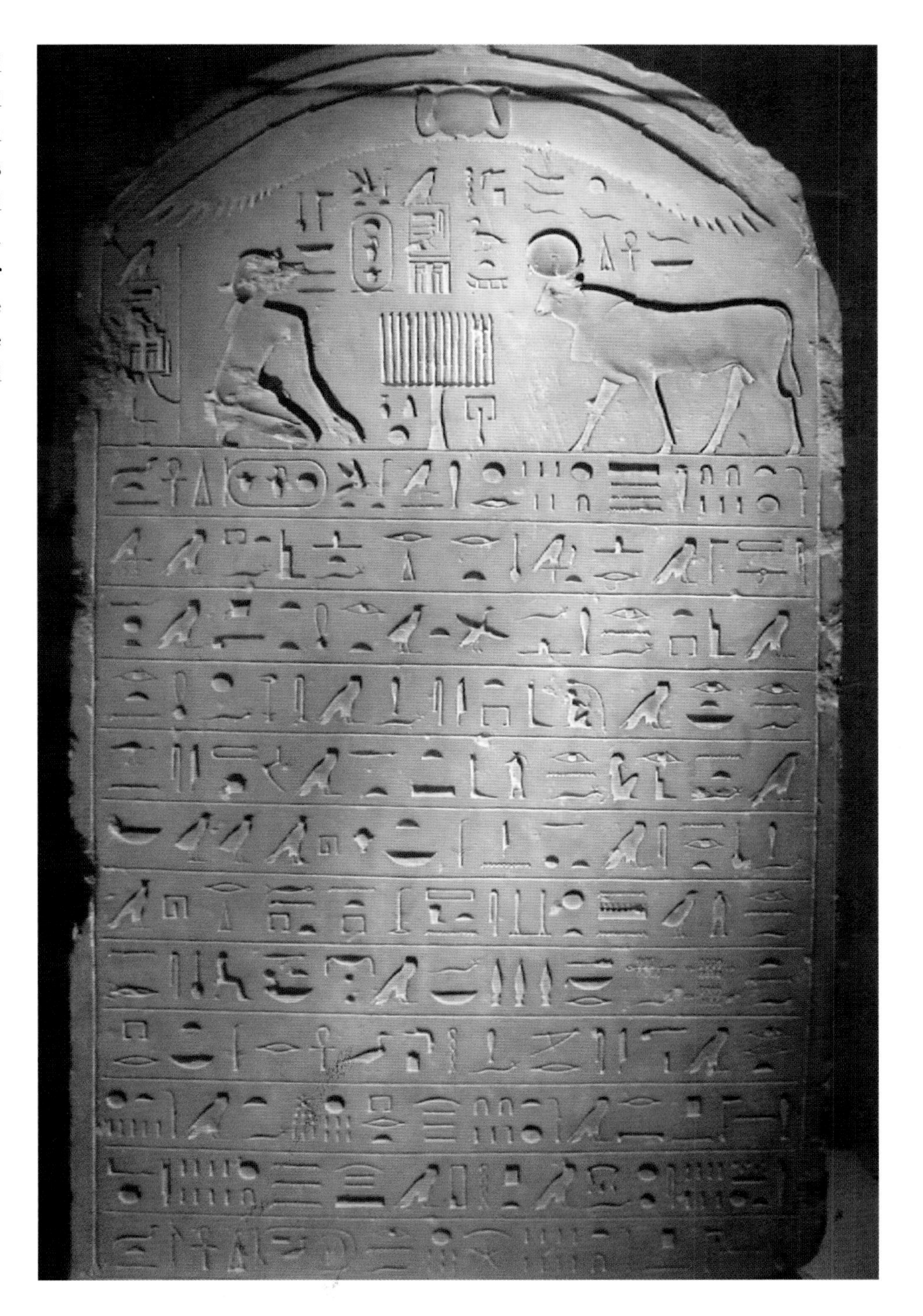

Above left: This fragment of a statue is of Ahmose II. He wears the traditional headgear of a pharaoh, with the snake motif on top. *(Jo St Mart)*

Left: Ahmose II was responsible for many building projects, in both Egypt and in neighboring countries and during his reign Egypt fostered a more cosmopolitan attitude. *(Jo St Mart)*

Right: This stele, now exhibited in the Louvre, Paris, dates back to the twenty-third year of Ahmose II's reign. *(Jo St Mart)*

The First Persian Period

Although the Greeks would describe the Persian conquest of Egypt as a bloodthirsty and cruel affair, filled with atrocities, the truth seems somewhat more sedate. Once Cambyses II had defeated the Egyptian army in 525 BCE, he took little interest in Egyptian affairs and, following his return to Persia, Egypt was ruled from afar under the supervision of Persian satraps.

Darius I succeeded Cambyses I in 522 BCE and held a tighter rein over the internal affairs of his conquered country, building new temples and repairing the old. He even completed the canal began by Necto II, joining the Eastern Delta to the Red Sea.

All in all, it was a prosperous time for Egypt. Revolution was inevitable, though, and in 486 BCE, the year of Darius I's death, the people rose up against their invaders. The new king, Xerxes, quickly quelled the rebels and left his son Achaemenes in charge. His cruelty to the people under his care fueled the flame of revolution once more, so when Xerxes was killed, his successor Artaxexes I was beset by the guerrilla tactics of Prince Amyrtaeus of Sais and the son of Psammthicus III, Inaros. The rebels were once again

defeated and Inaros was put to death. After that there followed thirty years of peace.

With the reign of Darius II in 423 BCE, trouble began again, centered around the important Delta families of Sais. Eventually, during the reigns of the final two Persian kings, Darius II and Artaxerxes II, Egypt gained a kind of semi-independence thanks to the in-fighting between the Persian royal family.

Left: Picturing Darius I of Persia, this stele is now in the Iran Museum and shows the king with his many servants. (*Jo St Mart*)

Above: Persepolis, the ancient capital of the Persian Empire, boasts many fine sculptures within its ruined walls. These depict the pharaoh Xerxes I. (*Jo St Mart*)

Hakor (Achoris)

393 BCE–380 BCE
29th Dynasty

The origins of Hakor are unknown but what is clear is that he rose to power following a struggle between the son of the previous king, Nepherites, and another man seeking to commandeer the throne. Despite having no legitimate claim on the monarchy, he expended a great deal of effort in creating a fictional relationship between himself and the preceding king. On his monuments he recorded his close relationship to the monarch and even named his son after him. Experts consider such blatant obsequiousness a clear sign that Hakor had made them all up. During his reign he commissioned a great deal of construction and renovation. He also managed to repel several Persian attacks on Egypt, thanks to the assistance of Greek mercenaries and a much stronger Egyptian navy. He died in 380 BCE but his son did not succeed him and was overthrown by Nectenbo I, the founder of the 30th Dynasty.

Below: These basalt sphinxes date to the 29th Dyansty and represent Hakor and his father Nepherites I. (*The Art Archive/Musée du Louvre, Paris/Gianni Dagli Orti/AA390317*)

Nectanebo II

360–343 BCE
30th Dynasty

Nectanebo II enjoyed a quiet reign for the first eight years after his succession. This was mainly due to Persia, Egypt's biggest threat, dealing with its own internal power struggles. However, when Artaxerxes III became the new Persian ruler in 350 BCE he immediately turned his attention to regaining control of his empire, including Egypt. At first he was unsuccessful but continued nevertheless. By 343 BCE the Persian and Egyptian armies met outside Pelusium, the stronghold of the Eastern Delta and a gateway into the rest of the country. This time the Persians were victorious, and soon marched across the rest of Egypt with little difficulty. Nectanebo II escaped to Nubia and was never heard of again.

Right: Standing astride a small Nectanebo II is a Horus falcon, wearing both the Upper and Lower Egypt crowns. (*Jo St Mart*)

The Macedonian Kings

The period following Alexander the Great's entry into Egypt was, like the pharaoh himself, short-lived but illustrious. Welcomed into the country as a liberator from the Persian yoke in 332 BCE, Alexander proceeded to lavish attention on his new conquest, restoring temples and monuments, founding Alexandria, which would later be the site of the greatest library the world had ever seen, and paying tribute to the Egyptian gods.

As part of his enormous empire, Egypt joined a wider community of nations and flourished, though along with the rest of his conquests it was plunged into turmoil at his death soon after (in 323 BCE). Ruled over by his mentally deficient half-brother Philip Arrhidaeus (323–317 BCE) and, after he was murdered, his son Alexander IV (317–305 BCE), it was not until Ptolemy I, the son of his childhood friend, claimed the throne that Egypt was returned to a semblance of stability.

Left: The frieze from the Temple of Amun at Luxor shows Alexander making an offering to the god Amun. (*Jo St Mart*)

Above: Although Alexander the Great did not stay long in Egypt, his impact on the country was enormous. (*Jo St Mart*)

Ptolemy I Soter
305–282 BCE

One of Alexander the Great's most respected and faithful generals, Ptolemy I Soter was the founder of Ptolemaic Egypt. He took the position of satrap of Egypt after he discovered that the previous ruler appointed by Alexander, Cleomenes, had stolen money from the temples and misappropriated funds designated for the army's wages. Ptolemy had the fraudster executed and took over the position. Following the death of Alexander, the country lay in turmoil, with many of his generals waging wars against each other and grabbing power wherever they could. Thanks to his prowess in battle, and smart diplomatic maneuverings, Ptolemy added Palestine and lower Syria to the Egyptian empire, and the country flourished. He ensured the continuation of the royal bloodline by taking the daughter of Nectanebo II, Eurydice, as his wife. He also married one of her ladies in waiting, Berenice, who bore him Ptolemy II Philadelius, his successor.

Right: A bust depicting Ptolemy I Soter, who had been a boyhood friend of Alexander the Great. (*Jo St Mart*)

Ptolemy II Philadelius

283–246 BCE

Three years before his death, Ptolemy I took his son as co-regent of Egypt. When his father died in 285 BCE, Ptomlemy II Philadelius took full control. Under his rule Egypt continued to prosper. His victories during the First Syrian War saw the expansion of his empire, from the Cyclades to Samathace, plus the coastal ports of Cilicia, Trachea, Lycia, and Caria. Egypt now boasted the most powerful navy in the east Mediterranean Sea. However, after losing many territories in the Second Syrian War, Ptolemy II agreed to a peace treaty with King Antiochus II Theos and as assurance gave him Berenice's, his daughter, hand in marriage. Ptolemy II had two wives. The first was Arsinoë I, daughter of Lysimachus, one of Alexander's finest generals. His next wife, whom he married after Arsinoë I, who was accused of treason and banished, was Arsinoë II. She was the widow of Lysimachus and Ptolemy's sister.

Left: This impressive statue portrays a regal Ptolemy II Philadelphus but differs greatly from other depictions of the pharaoh. (*Jo St Mart*)

Below: This grey granite bust of Ptolemy II would seem to be a more lifelike and realistic representation of the ruler. (*The Art Archive/Egyptian Museum, Cairo/Gianni Dagli Orti/AA389780*)

Ptolemy III Euergetes

246–222 BCE

Ptolemy III Euergetes and his siblings (a brother Lysimachus and a sister named Berenice) were raised by their step-mother and aunt, Arsinoë II. Ptolemy III did not take the throne until after the death of his father, by which time he was thirty years old. Not long after he came into power his sister asked him for help. Her husband had been poisoned by his jealous first wife, Laodice, and Berenice feared for the safety of herself and her son. Unfortunately, Ptolemy III could not reach her in time, and Berenice and her young son were murdered. In revenge he marched on northern Syria, occupied Antioch, and continued his campaign against Babylon for a further five years. However, Ptolemy was not merely a soldier. He also commissioned the building of a giant temple to Horus in Edfu, and founded the Serapeum in Alexandria, a huge temple dedicated to the patron god of Alexandria—Serapis.

Above: A marble bust of Ptolemy III Euergetes who ruled Egypt for 25 years. (*The Art Archive/Archaeological Museum, Venice/Alfredo Dagli Giannni/AA347908*)

Left: Ptolemy III is also credited with the construction of this massive stone gateway. (*Jo St Mart*)

Ptolemy IV Philapator

221–205 BCE

Unlike his father and grandfather, the fourth ruler of the Ptolemaic dynasty was a corrupt and weak man, easily led by others. During the first year of his rule he was persuaded, probably by Sosibius—a power-hungry Greek advisor and favorite of the king—to have his mother Berenice and brother Magus put to death. Berenice was poisoned and Magus was scalded to death, a barbaric yet fairly popular form of execution in those times.

Ptolemy IV had many vices and indulged them all, so much so that he allowed his favorites in the court to rule in his stead. Such lackluster leadership convinced the king of neighboring Syria, Antiochus III, that Egypt would be an easy target. Indeed, Antiochus took many Egyptian cities easily and, if Ptolemy IV had not secured a month-long truce, might have taken much of the country. During this truce Ptolemy and Sosibius decided to arm and train the people of Egypt, and when hostilities began anew Antiochus was defeated. Unfortunately for Ptolemy, the people of Egypt now recognized just how strong they were and began a revolt. This brought about the

Above: A silver coin bearing the profile of Ptolemy IV Philopator. *(The Art Archive/British Museum/ AA347953)*

Right: This later coin shows a much older version of Ptolemy IV. *(Jo St Mart)*

establishment of "Upper Egypt," a kingdom with its own pharaohs that lasted twenty years.

Ptolemy married his sister Arsinoë and had one son before another woman caught his eye: Agathoclea who, in collusion with her brothers Agathocles and Sosibius, pandered to all of the king's excesses. It is more than likely that this brought about his death aged just forty-one years.

Above: This frieze, dating to the reign of Ptolemy IV Philopator, shows the pharaoh making an offering to the gods Maat and Montu. *(Jo St Mart)*

Far right: What remains of the Rosetta Stone, a decree from Ptolemy V listing various building projects and laws on taxes. It has been invaluable in helping decipher ancient hieroglyphs. *(Jo St Mart)*

Ptolemy V Epiphanes

204–181 BCE

When Ptolemy V Epiphanes came to the throne he was just five years old. His mother had already been poisoned by Agathocles and Sosibius, who feared that she would declare herself regent and thus take control of the country. Once she had been dispatched the scheming conspirators made themselves the official guardians of the boy-king and thus obtained the regency. However, all would not go according to their plan. War hero and popular military leader Tlepolemus was suspicious of the new regents and led a revolt. He and a mob of Alexandrians stormed the royal palace in the capital city. He rescued the king, and Agathocles, Sosibius, and Agathoclea were killed by an angry mob.

In later life Ptolemy V was a master sportsman and a renowned huntsman. Unfortunately, he was also tyrannical, vindictive and cruel. He viciously suppressed any rebellions by the native peoples and in one notorious incident gave his word of honor that any surrendering rebels would be unharmed—then proceeded to put them to death.

Ptolemy VI Philometor

180–145 BCE

One of three children (the others being his sister Cleopatra II and his brother Ptolemy VIII Physcon), Ptolemy VI Philometor was just six years old when he became king. His mother, Cleopatra I became his regent and for five years ruled with wisdom. She kept ties with Rome and refused to start a war with Syria. After her death in 176 BCE the role of guardian to the prince was seized by Eulaeus and Lenaeus, two corrupt and foolish civil servants. They declared war on Antiochus IV, and Egypt was resoundingly defeated.

Antiochus crowned himself king but, thanks to an intervention by Rome, abandoned his claim on the Egyptian throne. Egypt was then led by the three siblings. Philometor ruled from Memphis with his wife and sister; Cleopatra II and his brother ruled from Alexandria. When Antiochus once again tried to invade Egypt, Philometor appealed to the Roman Senate for help. They sent Caius

Left: A gold ring decorated with the profile of Ptolemy VI Philometor. (*Jo St Mart*)

Below: A gold coin of Ptolemy VI Philometor. (*The Art Archive/AA347981*)

Popilius Laenas, who forced Antiochus to leave, and declared Philometor the ruler of Egypt and his brother the ruler of Cyrenaica, the eastern coastal region of Libya. The remainder of Philometor's reign was peaceful and the country thrived. He died in 145 BCE in a battle against Alexander Balas, his daughter's immoral husband.

Above: The Kom Ombo Temple on the banks of the Nile was established by Ptolemy VI and dedicated to many gods, including Sobek the crocodile god, Horus, Hathor, and Khonsu. (*Egyptian Tourist Board*)

Ptolemy VII Neos Philopater

c. 145 BCE

It is unclear whether Ptolemy VII Neos Philopator, son of Cleopatra II and Ptolemy VI Philometor, ever reigned in Egypt. Cleopatra II, recently widowed and with very little protection now that most of her husband's armies were supporting Demetrius II in the battle with Balas, sought help from her youngest brother, Ptolemy VIII Physcon. Seeing his chance to control all of Egypt, he arranged for his sister and his nephew to take refuge with him in Memphis. Despite their differences in the past, Cleopatra eventually agreed to become his wife. In this way she secured a safe future for her son. Regrettably, she underestimated how far her brother would go to secure his position; as soon as she gave birth to Physcon's heir, he murdered Ptolemy Neos Philopater.

Right: The stone carved will of the short-lived Ptolemy VII Neos Philapator. *(Jo St Mart)*

Ptolemy VIII Euergetes (also Physcon)

179–163 BCE and 145–116 BCE

Ptolemy VIII Euergetes was disliked by his people and given the unfortunate nickname of "physcon," meaning "pot belly," "sausage," or "bladder" in reference to his obesity. His rule was marred by bloodshed and deceit. Having married his sister and murdered her son he became infatuated with her daughter, Cleopatra III. She was eventually persuaded to marry him with the proviso that she also be named queen. So Egypt now had two queens, known as Sister Queen (Cleopatra II) and Wife Queen (Cleopatra III). The people of Egypt adored their "Sister Queen" because during, the rule of her first husband, Ptolemy VI, Egypt enjoyed a time of great prosperity and peace. This led to their dislike of Ptolemy VIII and his new wife heightening.

In fear of reprisals for his excesses, Ptolemy VIII Euergetes fled to Cyprus, taking his new wife and all of his children with him. He was just in time, as shortly after his departure an angry mob surged into the palace baying for his blood. Finding him gone, they set about destroying all his statues and anything that contained his image.

Safely in Cyprus, Euergetes planned his return to Egypt but was so angered by the destruction wrought by the angry mob and the fact that Cleopatra II, beloved by the people, now ruled in his stead, he slaughtered Memphites, the son they had together. In a cruel twist on the myth of Isis and Osiris, he sent the child's mutilated corpse to Cleopatra II as a birthday gift.

Euergetes eventually returned to Egypt in 129 BCE and regained his throne. Soon after, Cleopatra II fled to her daughter, now married to Demetrius II of Syria. She did however return to Egypt, although what happened to her on her return was never discovered. Euergetes died in 116 BCE and left the Egypt to Cleopatra III.

Right: Ptolemy VIII Euergetes II making an offering to the god Atum, from a relief at the Temple of Opet. (*The Art Archive/Gianni Dagli Orti/AA347981*)

Ptolemy XII Nios Dionysus

80–51 BCE

Ptolemy XII Nios Dionysus Theos Philopator Theos Philadelos took the throne of Egypt after the bloody death of Ptolemy XI Alexander II. The previous king ruled Egypt for only nineteen days before being lynched by an angry mob. He had unwisely killed his bride, Cleopatra Berenice, shortly after their wedding. She was beloved by her people and they rose up to avenge her death. There being no direct male heirs, the people turned to the illegitimate children of Ptolemy IX and an unknown Greek concubine. The eldest son was crowned king in 80 BCE. He ruled with his daughter, Cleopatra VI Teyphaena as co-regent and also his wife Cleopatra V.

He was the first pharaoh to understand the importance of a Roman alliance and worked hard to forge one. He bribed Julius Caesar and General Pompey in order to secure an alliance. Eventually, in 59 BCE Egypt was officially added to the list of Rome's friends but a year later relations had soured due to Ptolemy's lack of diplomacy, and he was forced to travel to Rome to plead his case for the throne. In his absence, Berenice IV, his daughter, was crowned ruler.

He finally won back his throne in 55 BCE by paying Aulus Gabinius, a famous Roman general and statesman, to invade Egypt. Berenice was executed shortly afterwards. Ptolemy XII ruled peacefully until he became seriously ill in 51 BCE. He named Cleopatra VII and her brother Ptolemy XIII as his successors and made Rome the executors of his will.

Right: King Ptolemy XII, the father of Cleopatra VII. (*Jo St Mart*)

Far right: The carved exterior walls of the Temple of Horus at Edfu, showing Ptolemy XII Neos making offerings to gods. (*The Art Archive/Gianni Dagli Orti/AA396578*)

Cleopatra VII

51–30 BCE

Undoubtedly the best known of all the Egyptian queens, Cleopatra VII Thea Philopater came to power with her husband—and brother Ptolemy XIII—in 51 BCE. A savvy political leader and an expert seductress, she used her brain and her body to solidify her grip on the throne. Her life has been immortalized in films, paintings, and books and her political machinations, her important lovers and eventual fall are worthy of them all.

When King Ptolemy XIII took the throne he was only ten years old, so his older sister and wife, Cleopatra, took control of the country. She was just seventeen. The Romans were still considering the annexation of Egypt and had an army stationed within their borders, so when Cleopatra decided to lend her support to General Pompey, the arch-rival of Julius Caesar, her people and her king turned against her. When she learned that her husband was plotting to have her killed, she fled to the east. Safely away from Ptolemy, she began raising an army and plotted to recapture her throne. By 48 BCE the rival armies of Ptolemy and Cleopatra were ready to go to war.

Not sure of gaining victory, Ptolemy sought help from Rome. He arranged the assassination of General Pompey in the hope he could secure the good favor of Julius Caesar. When Caesar arrived in Alexandria that same year he summoned the warring couple to the royal palace. It was here that Ptolemy offered him the preserved hand of his greatest enemy, Pompey. Unfortunately the plan backfired and Caesar backed Cleopatra's claim to the throne.

Despite having the official backing of Rome, the rest of Egypt had other ideas. They rejected Cleopatra and turned to the youngest royal sister, Arsinoe IV, and crowned her the new queen of Egypt. Meanwhile, Caesar and Cleopatra were trapped and barricaded inside the royal palace of

Left: An intricate carving of Cleopatra VII, in which she appears youthful and happy. (*Jo St Mart*)

Alexandria. From November 48 BCE to March 47 BCE they remained stranded, and by the time Roman troops arrived to rescue them, they were not only political allies but also lovers.

Now that his wife was free and had the army of Rome behind her, Ptolemy fled. Unfortunately, he drowned while trying to cross the River Nile. At the same time, the newly crowned Arsinoe was imprisoned then transported to Rome.

Suddenly widowed and pregnant with Caesar's child, Cleopatra married her eleven-year-old brother, Ptolemy XIV. In November 47 BCE she gave birth to a son and named him Ptolemy Caesar after his father (he was generally known as Caesarion). The arrival of the child further cemented the bond between Rome and Egypt. Caesar and Cleopatra would have a joint interest in the welfare and future of their son. Also, Egypt could remain independent (meaning their son could one day inherit the thrones of both Egypt and Rome), and the country could enjoy the protection of the most powerful country in the world.

In return, Rome would receive

Left: An arresting statue thought to represent the seductive Cleopatra VII. *(Jo St Mart)*

generous gifts from one of the most bountiful countries on the globe. Even when Caesar had left Egypt, he still remained loyal to Cleopatra and supported her right to the throne of Egypt. As Caesar already had a wife in Rome, he could not officially recognize Caesarion as his son, although shortly before his death he did try to pass a law through the Senate that would allow him to take a second wife and child in another country.

While waiting for this new legislation to pass, Cleopatra, her son and her husband, Ptolemy, traveled to Rome and lived in Caesar's private manor for over a year. In 44 BCE Caesar was assassinated. A distraught Cleopatra and her entourage immediately returned home. It is unclear whether it was by accident or design, but shortly after her return, Cleopatra was once again a widow following the convenient death of Ptolemy XIV. With no other male heir in line Caesarion, now three years old, was crowned king. This meant that once again Cleopatra was the real ruler of Egypt. To be sure of her and her son's position she would first have to rid herself of the competition – Arsinoe. Having escaped f rom Rome and now living in Ephesus, Arsinoe was plotting with the ruler of Cyprus over the recapture of the Egyptian throne. In 40 BCE, Arsinoe was murdered on Cleopatra's command.

Back in Rome, Mark Antony, Octavian (soon to be Emperor Augustus), and Marcus Lepidus had joined forces to track down the assassins of Julius Caesar—Brutus and Cassius. Naturally, Cleopatra volunteered her forces to the search and the killers were soon hunted down and dispatched.

Rome itself was in turmoil following Caesar's death. It was now split into two parts, the eastern and western empires. Octavian, the rightful heir, held the west and Mark Antony ruled the east. Such a position was unsustainable; Rome must have but one ruler.

Egypt was also left vulnerable after Julius Caesar's demise. Cleopatra had to ally herself to one of these rulers to ensure the safety of her country. For the first time in her life as queen she made a disastrous decision. She chose Mark Antony. More a soldier than a political animal, he lacked the cunning and guile of Caesar. Once again, using her undoubted charms, she seduced Mark Antony, her new protector. By 40 BCE she had given birth to twins, named Cleopatra Selene and Alexander Helios. Mark Antony's wife (and also sister to Octavian) was less than pleased. The relationship between her, her husband, and her brother began to sour.

This very public humiliation of his sister and some disastrous military campaigns by Mark Antony led to Octavian's increasing impatience with his co-ruler. The final straw came when, following a decisive victory in Armenia, Antony commemorated the occasion in Alexandria by sitting on a golden throne and announcing himself and his sons as the true kings of Rome and Egypt, and Caesarion the rightful heir to Caesar. Octavian went to war against Antony and won. He fled to Alexandria to join Cleopatra. Again she found herself trapped inside the royal palace but this time without any hope of rescue. She offered to abdicate the throne so that her children might take her place, but to no avail.

Antony had little choice but to fight. He left the palace for the battlefields and Cleopatra barricaded herself in her treasury. When Mark Antony heard the news that Cleopatra had committed suicide he threw himself on his sword. In a terrible twist of fate, he had been misinformed and a mortally wounded Antony was dragged back to the palace to die in the arms of his queen. All was lost for Cleopatra. On August 12, 30 BCE she took her own life. It is widely believed that she was bitten by an asp, its deadly poison putting an end to the last queen of Egypt.

Ptolemy XV Caesarion

36–30 BCE

The last king of the Ptolemaic dynasty, Ptolemy Philopator Philometor Caesar was born in 47 BCE, son to Cleopatra and Julius Caesar. Although he co-ruled with his mother from 44 BCE to 30 BCE, it is unlikely, considering his age, that he ever truly ruled Egypt.

Following his mother's and step-father's suicides Caesarion, now seventeen years old, was rushed to the Red Sea, perhaps in hopes that he could to flee to India. Unfortunately, he was betrayed by the people meant to be protecting him and he was delivered to Octavian in Alexandria. Sadly, the last king of Egypt met his death in the city. Octavian executed the boy with the famous words, "Two Caesars is one too many."

Right: Cleopatra VII and her son, Caesarion, appear on a relief on the back wall of the Temple of Hathor in Dendera, where they are making offerings to the gods. (*Jo St Mart*)

Chronology

DYNASTY 0
3100–2920 BCE.

Narmer
c. 3150 BCE.

c. 3100 Reunification of Upper and Lower Egypt.
c. 3100 First hieroglyphic scripts appear.

EARLY DYNASTIC PERIOD

1ST DYNASTY

Hor-Aha
c. 3050 BCE

Hor-Aha founds the capital city of Memphis.

Djer
c. 3040 BCE

c. 3040 BCE Djer establishes Memphis.

Djet
c. 3008–3005 BCE

c. 3000 BCE Earliest recorded attempts of mummification.

Den
c. 3005–2973 BCE

Anedjib
c. 2973– 2970 BCE

Semerkhet
c. 2970–2955 BCE

Mining begins in the Sinai.

Qa'a
c. 2955–2929 BCE

2ND DYNASTY
2890–2686 BCE

Papyrus is used for the first time.

Hotepsekhemwy
c. 2890 BCE

Saqqara becomes official royal burial ground following the death of Hotepsekhemwy.

Raneb
c. 2860 BCE

Nynetjer
c. 2820 BCE

Seth-Peribsen
c. 2780 BCE

Khasekhemwy
c. 2760 BCE

OLD KINGDOM
2686–2181 BCE

3RD DYNASTY

Sanakhte
c. 2686–2668 BCE

Djoser
c. 2668–2649 BCE

Djoser's step pyramid, the first to be built entirely from stone, is completed at Saqqara and designed by the architect Imhotep.

Sekhemkhet
c. 2649–2643 BCE

Khaba
c. 2643–2637 BCE

Huni
c. 2637–2613 BCE

4TH DYNASTY

Snefru
c. 2613–2589 BCE

Snefru builds the Bent Pyramid and the Red Pyramid at Dahshur.

Khufu
c. 2589–2566 BCE

c. 2560 BCE Khufu completes the Great Pyramid at Giza after twenty years.

Djedefre
c. 2566–2558 BCE

Khafre
c. 2558–2532 BCE

Monument of the Great Sphinx erected to Khafre.

Menkaure
c. 2532–2504 BCE

Second largest pyramid at Giza completed for Khafre.

Third and smallest pyramid at Giza constructed for Menkaure.
Shepseskaf
c.2504–2500 BCE

5TH DYNASTY

Userkaf
c. 2498–2491 BCE

Sahure
c. 2491–2477 BCE

c. 2490 First expeditions sent overseas to Punt for the purpose of trade.

Neferirkare Kakai
c. 2477–2467 BCE

Shepseskare
c. 2467–2460 BCE

Neferefre
c. 2460–2453 BCE

Niuserre Ini
c. 2453–2422 BCE

Menkauhor
c. 2422–2414 BCE

c. 2420 BCE Work begins on the massive sun temple, Abu Gurab, at Abusir.

Djedkare Isesi
c. 2414–2375 BCE

Unas
c. 2375–2345 BCE

c. 2340 BCE Engraving of the Palermo Stone begins.

c. 2345 BCE Unas becomes the first of many pharaohs to incorporate "spells" in their funerary monuments.

Above: The White Chapel of Senusret I at Karnak has been reconstructed from old stone fragments. It was built to celebrate Senusret I's thirtieth jubilee. This relief was one of the few pieces found intact. (*Jo St Mart*)

6TH DYNASTY

Teti
c. 2345–2333 BCE

c. 2333 BCE The noblemen slowly begin to take power and wealth from the pharaoh.

Pepi I
c. 2332–2283 BCE

c. 2340 BCE Pepi I begins rebuilding the Osiris temple at Abydos.

Weni the Elder is named the first governor of Upper Egypt.

Merenre Nemtyemsaf I
c. 2283–2278 BCE

Pepi II
c. 2278–2184 BCE

c. 2184 BCE The fall of the Old Kingdom and the pharaoh loses control. Egypt is divided between several powerful nomarchs.

FIRST INTERMEDIATE PERIOD
2181–2060 BCE

THE MIDDLE KINGDOM
2060–1782 BCE

7TH AND 8TH DYNASTIES
c. 2181–2161 BCE

Wadjkare

Qakare Iby

9TH AND 10TH DYNASTIES
c. 2160–2040 BCE

Meryibre Khety

Merykare

Kaneferre

Nebkaure Akhtoy

11TH DYNASTY

Intef I
c. 2134–2117 BCE

Intef II
c. 2117–2069 BCE

Intef III
c. 2069–2060 BCE
Mentuhotep I
2060–2010 BCE

Mentuhotep I reunites Upper and Lower Egypt.

Thebes becomes the capital city for most of the 11th Dynasty.

Mentuhotep II
c. 2010–1998 BCE

Mentuhotep III
c. 1997–1991 BCE

12TH DYNASTY

Amenemhet I
1991–1962 BCE

Amenemhet I builds a new capital city called Itjtawy, thought to be present-day el-Lisht.

Senusret I
c. 1971–1926 BCE
Southern Nubia falls under Egyptian control.

Amenemhet II
c. 1929–1895 BCE

Senusret II
c. 1897–1878 BCE

Work begins on irrigating the Faiyum Oasis area.

Senusret III
c. 1878–1841 BCE

The canal at First Cataract is made navigable by boat.
Amenemhet III
c. 1842–1797 BCE

The first built at Dahshur, the Black Pyramid is completed for Amenemhet III.

Amenemhet IV
c. 1798–1786 BCE

Queen Sobeknefru
c. 1785–1782 BCE

THE SECOND INTERMEDIATE PERIOD
1782–1574 BCE

The Hyksos invade and conquer the eastern Delta.

13TH DYNASTY

Wegaf
c. 1782–1780 BCE

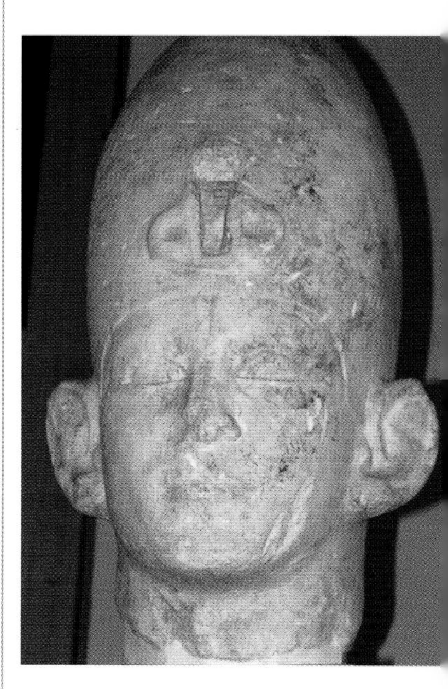

Above: This white bust of Senusret III now resides in the Luxor Museum, Egypt. (*Jo St Mart*)

Above: Once again displaying Akhenaten's singular looks, this relief in Luxor shows the pharaoh making an offering to the sun god, Ra. *(Jo St Mart)*

Sobekhotep I
c. 1766 BCE

Ameny Intef IV
c. 1770–1760 BCE

Hor I
c. 1760 BCE

Sobekhotep II
c. 1750 BCE

Khendjer
c. 1747 BCE

Sobekhotep III
c. 1745 BCE

Neferhotep I
c. 1741–1730 BCE

Sobekhotep IV
c. 1730–1720 BCE

Ay
c. 1720 BCE

Neferhotep II
c. 1710 BCE

15TH DYNASTY
1663–1555 BCE

Sheshi

Yakubher

Khyan

Apepi I

Apepi II

16TH DYNASTY
1663–1555 BCE

Anather

Yakobaam

17TH DYNASTY

Intef VI
c. 1620 BCE

Tao I
c. 1633

Tao II
c. 1574 BCE

Kamose
c. 1573–1570 BCE

Conflicts begin between the nobles of Thebes and the Hyksos king, Apepi Awoserre.

THE NEW KINGDOM
1570–1070 BCE

18TH DYNASTY

c. 1500 BCE This period sees the introduction of the horse-drawn chariot.

Ahmose I
c. 1570–1546 BCE

The Hyksos are ousted from the Delta and central power is restored to Thebes, the new capital city.

The first attempts at glass making begin.

An official civil service is founded by Ahmose I.

Amenhotep I
c. 1551–1524 BCE

Below: A fragment of a statue depicting Ahmose I. This painted bust shows the pharaoh wearing the high crown of Upper Egypt. *(Jo St Mart)*

Valley of the Kings becomes the primary burial ground for the pharaohs.

The first water clock is invented.

The first copy of the Amduat, the book describing what to expect in the underworld, is completed.

Thutmose I
c. 1524–1518 BCE

Thutmose I begins the construction of the temple at Karnak.

Egypt conquers Nubia.

Thutmose II
c. 1518–1504 BCE

c. 1518 A short rebellion at Kush is quickly quashed.

Hatshepsut
c. 1479–1458 BCE

The remarkable mortuary complex at Der el-Bahri is constructed.

Thutmose III
c. 1504–1450 BCE

Amenhotep II
c. 1453–1419 BCE

Thutmose IV
c. 1419–1386 BCE

Amenhotep III
c. 1386–1349 BCE

Akhenaten (Amenhotep IV)
c. 1350–1334 BCE

Akenhaten attempts to change religious practices of Egypt to monotheistic worship of Aten, god of the sun.

Smenkhkare
c. 1336–1334 BCE

Tutenkhamun
c. 1333–1324 BCE

Tutenkhamun restores the original religions and reopens the temples.

Horemheb
c. 1321_1293 BCE

19TH DYNASTY

Ramesses I
c. 1293–1291 BCE

Seti I
c. 1291–1278 BCE

Seti begins building the Great Hypostle Hall in Karnak.

Ramesses II
c. 1279–1212 BCE

c. 1274 BCE Ramesses II fights at the Battle of Kadesh, the largest battle ever fought on chariots.

Merneptah
c. 1212–1202 BCE

Amenmesses
c. 1202–1199 BCE

Seti II
c. 1199–1193 BCE

Siptah
c. 1193–1187 BCE

Queen Twosret
c. 1187–1185 BCE

20TH DYNASTY

Setnakhte
c. 1185–1182 BCE

Ramesses III
c. 1182–1151 BCE

Ramesses IV
c. 1151–1145 BCE

Ramesses V
c. 1145–1141 BCE

Ramesses VI
c. 1141–1133 BCE

Ramesses VII
c. 1133–1126 BCE

Ramesses VIII
c. 1133–1126 BCE

Ramesses IX
c. 1126–1108 BCE

Ramesses X
c. 1108–1098 BCE

Ramesses XI
c. 1098–1070 BC

Herihor
c. 1080–1074 BCE

Above: An aerial view of Medinet Habu, the mortuary temple of Ramesses III. It contains detailed descriptions of Ramesses III's many victories, including his war against the Sea Peoples. (*Jo St Mart*)

Above: The "Gate of All Nations" in Persepolis was once a giant covered hallway measuring 82 feet square. (*Jo St Mart*)

THIRD INTERMEDIATE PERIOD
1070–525 BCE

21ST DYNASTY

Smendes I
c. 1069–1043 BCE

Amenemnisu
c. 1043–1039 BCE

Psusennes I
c. 1039–991 BCE

Amenemope
c. 993–984 BCE

Osorkon the Elder
c. 984–978 BCE

Siamun
c. 978–959 BCE

Psusennes II
c. 959–945 BCE

22ND DYNASTY
(Libyan Dynasty based in Tanis)

Sheshonq I
c. 945–924 BCE

Osorkon I
c. 924–889 BCE

Sheshonq II
c. 890 BCE

Takelot I
c. 889–874 BCE

Osorkon II
c. 874–850 BCE

Takelot II
c. 850–825 BCE

Sheshonq III
c. 825–773 BCE

Pami
c. 773–730 BCE

Sheshonq V
c. 767–730 BCE

Osorkon IV
c. 730–715 BCE

23RD DYNASTY
(based at Leontopolis)

Pedibastet
c. 818–793 BCE

Sheshonq IV
c. 793–787 BCE

Osorkon III
c. 787–759 BCE

Takelot III
c. 764–757 BCE

Rudamon
c. 757–754 BCE

Iuput
c. 754–715 BCE

24TH DYNASTY
(based in Sais)

Tefnakht
c. 727–720 BCE

Bakenrenef
c. 720–715 BCE

25TH DYNASTY
(Nubian Dynasty)

Piankhi
c. 747–716 BCE

Below: This painting by Franciszek Smuglewicz is called "Scythians Meeting with Darius" and was completed in 1785. (*Jo St Mart*)

Above: An example of an old coin dating back to the rule, and bearing the profile, of Ptolemy V Epiphanes. (*The Art Archive/British Museum/ AA347954*)

c. 728 BCE Piy, the Nubian king, begins his rule of Egypt, establishing a Nubian Dynasty.

Shabaka
c. 716–702 BCE

Shebitku
c. 702–690 BCE

Taharqa
c. 690–664 BCE

669 BCE The Assyrians successfully invade Egypt.

Tanutamun
c. 664–656 BCE

THE LATE PERIOD
525–332 BCE

26TH DYNASTY

Psammethicus I
664–610 BCE

Nekau
610–595 BCE
Psammethicus II
595–589 BCE

Wahibre
589–570 BCE

Ahmose II
570–526 BCE

Psammethicus III
526–525 BCE

525 BCE The Persians invade Egypt.

28TH DYNASTY

Amyrtaeus
404–399 BCE

29TH DYNASTY

Mendes becomes the new capital city.

Nefaarud I
399–393 BCE

Hakor
393–380 BCE

30TH DYNASTY

Nectanebo I
380–362 BCE

Djedhor
362–360 BCE

Nectanebo II
360–343 BCE

332 BCE Alexander the Great conquers Egypt.

331 BCE Alexander the Great founds the new capital city of Alexandria.

PTOLEMAIC PERIOD
305–30 BCE

Ptolemy I Soter
305–282 BCE

Ptolemy II Philadelius
283–246 BCE

Ptolemy III Euergetes
246–222 BCE

Ptolemy IV Philapator
221–205 BCE

Ptolemy V Epiphanes
204–181 BCE

196 BCE Carving of the Rosetta Stone begins.
Ptolemy VI Philometor
180–145 BCE

Ptolemy VII Neos Philopater
c. 145 BCE

Ptolemy VIII Euergetes II
170–163 BCE, 145–116 BCE

Ptolemy XII Nios Dionysus.
80–51 BCE

Cleopatra VII
51–30 BCE

31 BCE Battle of Actium. Egypt loses and becomes part of the Roman Empire.

Ptolemy XV Caesarion
36–30 BCE

Below: This relief, found on the northern wall of the Esna Temple, is remarkably well preserved and depicts Ptolemy VI alongside many of the major Egyptian gods. (*Jo St Mart*)

Index